The
Essential
Guide to
Bullying

Jennifer Thomson

Published in Great Britain in 2018 by
need2know
Remus House
Coltsfoot Drive
Peterborough
PE2 9BF
Telephone 01733 898103
www.need2knowbooks.co.uk

Contents

Introduction

'Former pupil sues over bullying'.

'Bullying link to child suicide rate, charity suggests'.

'Boy jumps to his death after being bullied on Facebook'.

'School did nothing to stop bullying.'

'Girl jailed for bullying on Facebook'.

It seems that you can't pick up a newspaper these days or turn on the TV without hearing about how the lives of children are being made a misery by bullies. The headlines are everywhere and, alarmingly for parents, often schools have been made aware of the bullying and haven't always done everything in their power to stop it.

It's no wonder that parents are worried about bullying and have so many questions:

- How will they know if their child is being targeted?
- What is cyberbullying and how can they keep their child safe online?
- What can they do about the bullying if it's happening?
- Is their child's school fulfilling its obligations towards their child?
- How can they make their bullied child feel better about themselves?

It's time to sort out the facts from the fiction and to get to the crux of the matter.

School days are supposed to be the happiest of your life, but try telling that to the thousands of children who phone ChildLine and charities like it every year because they are being bullied and just can't take it anymore. For them school is something to dread. Knowing your child is suffering is every parent's worst nightmare.

These days, bullying is not just something that happens in school. Sadly, the popularity of social networking on the Internet on sites like Facebook and Twitter has given bullies a new platform from which they can taunt their victims. The fact that so many children now have mobile phones with Internet access means that the bullying may never end unless they switch their phones off; something they are loathe to do.

'It seems that you can't pick up a newspaper these days or turn on the TV without hearing about how the lives of children are being made a misery by bullies.'

In 2009, Keeley Haughton from Worcester, became the first person in the UK to be jailed for bullying on a social network site after she posted a death threat.

Could your child be one of the children being bullied?

The good news is that bullying can be stopped. No one has to put up with it.

The government has recognised that bullying is such a huge problem that by law schools must have a bullying policy and when you complain to them they have to do something about it. Not every parent is aware of a school's obligations to its pupils, so that will be covered in great detail in this book.

And even the rich and famous are helping to beat the scourge of bullying. Kate Middleton, who suffered from bullying herself (she was forced to leave her private school at 13 because of bullying), asked her wedding guests to donate to the anti-bullying charity Beatbullying. Flamboyant pop star, Lady Gaga has also spoken out about her experiences. British diving champion, Tom Daley was forced to leave his school after he was targeted by jealous bullies.

'Like anyone who has been bullied, Britain's newest princess and celebrities know about the damage that bullying can do.'

Like anyone who has been bullied, Britain's newest princess and celebrities know about the damage that bullying can do. How it goes right to the core of a child's being and can ruin their chances of enjoying life and getting the qualifications for the career that they want.

I also know what it's like. As a bully survivor, I've been there. I've had chewing gum stuck in my hair and a lit match held so close to my face it singed my hair. I've had my head shoved down the loo and flushed and been thrown into broken glass. I've had a boy come up to me on the school bus and stick his head in my face and spit 'Ugly' as every other kid watched. He was so close I could see the tiny scratch on his chin. I've been called 'useless' and had a host of insults hurled at me that I couldn't possibly repeat and I've cried myself to sleep at night and prayed that I wouldn't wake up again and have to leave the house.

I didn't tell anyone about the bullying at the time and it lasted for six very long years. It wasn't until I was older and the bullying seemed like a lifetime away, that I realised that's where bullies get all their power from – their target suffering in silence. If no one knows anything is wrong, how can they do anything about it?

That's why one of the main objectives of this book is to get your child to confide in you, because when you know something is wrong you can do something about it. The bully loses their power.

The natural response to the news that your child is being bullied is one of anger and of despair. It's often a case of, 'Why did I not know it was happening, does my child not trust me enough to tell me?'. Parents feel that their children should be able to come to them with their problems and that they should be able to protect their children against anything and everything. It may come as a great shock to discover that just because you are a parent that you aren't Superwoman or Superman; that you can't keep your child completely safe and that no, they won't always confide in you.

Then it's a case of what can I do?

The first thing anyone can do for a bullied child is to say, 'It's not your fault you're being bullied.' That is the single most important thing any parent can say to their child.

When I was being bullied I believed that I was weak and a coward. I was too different. I didn't like the same stuff as other kids. I smiled too much. I didn't smile enough. I bounced when I walked. (Crazy as it may sound, I actually did believe that it was because I bounced when I walked.) Chances are that your child will feel that way too and it won't be a case of there's something wrong with the bully, it's, 'There's something wrong with me.' They need reassurance that's not so.

That's another aim of this book – to stop your child from blaming themselves for being bullied and to help build their self-esteem; something that bullying eats away at like a cancer.

There's another person who needs to stop blaming themselves if their child is being bullied, and that's you. No parent can be with their child 24 hours a day, seven days a week. It just isn't possible. And you can't always notice the warning signs, especially when you don't even know what they are.

All parents can do is to equip themselves with the knowledge and tools needed to help their children in every way they can to deal with their problems, whether it's bullying or anything else. And that means getting clued-up on the issues that affect them, like bullying. It's time to tackle bullying…

'All parents can do is to equip themselves with the knowledge and tools needed to help their children in every way they can.'

Bullying: The Inside Story

Parents are quite rightly worried about the bullying culture that seems to be part of children growing up. Bullying is a problem that has been in the headlines constantly. Such is the extent of the problem that there have even been calls to criminalise bullying. The government are just as concerned and since September 1999 every school must have an anti-bullying policy by law.

When you're a parent it can be easy to panic when you read these nightmare stories of bullying that drove children to take their own lives and to wonder if your child could be suffering at the hands of bullies as many children are. Are you worrying unnecessarily?

It's time to go beyond the headlines and to find out just how widespread bullying is.

The facts

Statistics show that most children will have some experience of bullying. That doesn't necessarily mean that they themselves will become a victim of a prolonged campaign by a bully or bullies. They may, for instance, have witnessed bullying. But, sadly for many children, it does mean they have been bullied as these facts show:

- There have been calls for Facebook to put a panic button on their site after accusations of bullying. In some cases, children have attempted to take their lives after being bullied online.

- A staggering 32,562 children and young people called ChildLine in 2007 and 2008 to talk about being bullied.

- According to the information gathered by the NSPCC Child Protection Awareness and Diversity Department in December 2007, 31% of children were bullied by their peers during childhood.

- In a recent government survey, a quarter of children questioned admitted that they were sometimes afraid to go to school because of bullying.

- In a 2008 survey carried out on behalf of Ofsted (The Office for Standards in Education), 44% of children and young people said they had been bullied at school.

- The government recognised how bad the problem of bullying in schools has become, and schools in England and Wales were given powers to exclude pupils who persistently bully.

- Every year there is an Anti-bullying Week. In 2011 it will be from the 14th to the 18th of November and the focus will be on verbal bullying.

What is bullying?

It's important that bullying is defined because quite often those who are being bullied are accused of being oversensitive. 'You can't take a joke,' is often the line of choice for bullies who want to defend their actions. What we need to know is when does the playful teasing that kids do, cross over into something far more serious that we call bullying?

You could spend all day wracking your brains coming up with a definition that will fit perfectly and then someone else will come up with one that fits just as well.

'When you're a parent it can be easy to panic when you read these nightmare stories of bullying that drove children to take their own lives and to wonder if your child could be suffering at the hands of bullies as many children are. Are you worrying unnecessarily?'

The general definition I like to use is:

Bullying is basically when someone does or says something deliberately intended to cause hurt or embarrassment to their target.

There are many different definitions for bullying. You could also say:

- Bullying is when someone steals your property and either won't give it back or breaks or vandalises it in some way. This usually happens more than once. This can be anything from writing all over someone's school books to grabbing their mobile phone and refusing to hand it over.

- Bullying is when someone intentionally calls you names or insults you to make you feel bad. This can be done verbally or on a social networking site like Facebook.

- Bullying is when someone hits you or throws something at you, not because they have lost their temper, but because they have set out to hurt you.

- Bullying is when someone threatens to hurt you or even kill you. Note: Sending someone death threats is a criminal offence. If that happens to your child, go to the police with the evidence. If it's written down take that. If it's online, try and get a screen grab of the offending message. Ask someone for help if you don't know how to do this.

- Bullying is when you are left out of a group and treated like you don't exist. This can be in person or online. This type of bullying can be every bit as damaging as someone physically hurting your child.

- Bullying is when you are sent text messages saying nasty things about you that may also be sent to others. For example, everybody listed in the senders' contact list.

- Bullying is when someone posts an unflattering picture of you online. For example, a photo that was taken when you fell off your bike and were crying, and circulates it to others on Facebook.

With bullying, the pattern usually repeats itself. Bullying is rarely a one-off event. It can go on for days, weeks, months and even years.

Whatever the definition of bullying, or the form it takes, bullying is aimed at singling the target out, ruining the target's confidence, making them feel depressed and as though they don't belong. Bullies enjoy watching their targets suffer.

What bullying is not:

- Sometimes kids can say things to other children that aren't intended to hurt them and, although a bit insensitive and thoughtless, this would not be considered bullying. A clear distinction has to be made.

- Someone being a bit rough when they are playing and accidentally hurting someone. They didn't deliberately set out to cause hurt. Bullying is all about intention.

- Children having an argument or falling out: kids argue and fall out all the time. It doesn't mean someone is being bullied.

- A difference of opinion on a message board. Just because children disagree doesn't mean it's bullying.

Types of bullying

Bullying falls into two categories – the physical and the psychological. Bullying, especially over a prolonged period of time, often combines the two.

For example, kids who are being called names may also be kicked and punched and be tripped up.

There's a common misconception that bullying is only bullying when it involves violence or the threat of it, but psychological bullying can be just as traumatic as being assaulted. In fact, many bullied kids I talked to at the youth club where I used to volunteer, said that it was the effect on their minds and the attack on their sense of self that hurt far more than any physical scars. The impact on their minds was also more difficult to recover from even long after the bullying had stopped. That was my experience too.

'Our volunteer counsellors tell us that the calls they receive about bullying are some of the most painful they encounter.'

TV personality Esther Rantzen, ChildLine chairman.

The form bullying takes

Bullying has many guises. The behaviour of some pupils in our schools goes way beyond name-calling. Some kids are physically assaulted and subjected to what can only be described as systematic psychological abuse. Cyberbullying can get personal: criticising who a person is and how they look to the point that they have no confidence left.

Cyberbullying

With the explosion of the Internet has come new ways for bullies to target people, and that includes people they might not even have met.

Cyberbullying can be difficult to detect and takes many forms:

- Leaving nasty messages and comments on Facebook and other social networking sites.

- Making up lies about someone and spreading them around as though they were the truth.

- Getting into accounts and changing details, say like writing that someone wets the bed or has warts or changing their user name to something downright mean or nasty.

- Sending them abusive emails or messages calling them ugly, stupid or fat etc…

- Not including them in online groups although all of their friends are in them. This is a form of excluding them from their peers and making them feel like they have no friends.

- Posting nasty comments on your child's blog or their own about your child. This can be anything from making jokes up about them, to telling outright lies.

- Pretending to be someone they are not to make trouble, like pretending to be the boy your daughter has a crush on or their favourite soap star.

Tip:
You can block certain websites from being accessed from your home computer. Contact your Internet provider for details.

Case study

In 2011, bullies created a Facebook page for 10-year-old Blake Rice, who survived a flash flood in Australia which killed his brother (who died after insisting rescuers saved his younger brother first) and mother. They boasted about attacking him with sticks at a skateboard park.

Source – *The Age* newspaper.

Fact: In 2011, Thames Valley Police launched a pilot scheme in Reading to target bullying on Facebook with the help of cyberMentors, a site run by anti-bullying charity Beatbullying whose website can be found at www.beatbullying.org

Fact: In the last three months of 2010, Thames Valley Police recorded 800 cyberbullying offences in the region alone.

To view the CyberMentors site, go to www.cybermentors.org.uk. The site allows young people to talk to mentors online and is run by charity BeatBullying.

Tip:
It is possible to block numbers on mobile phones. Consult the manual that came with the phone for details or ask the network provider for details.

Mobile phone bullying

Sadly, with new technology comes new methods of bullies making other children's life hell. There have been documented instances where children have been bullied by mobile phone.

In extreme cases bullies have been caught using their mobile phones to send pictures of themselves attacking their victims to other bullies with some even being put onto websites to taunt and humiliate the people they cowardly attacked. This form of bullying, which is basically assault, was given the unfortunate title of 'happy slapping'.

Case study

Simon, 14, was a victim of text bullying: 'I was getting hassled at school by a gang and they got a hold of my mobile number. They began texting me telling me that they were going to beat me up when they got me alone. Once, they sent me a message saying that they were going to beat me up after school and steal all my clothes so I would have to go home naked. When I saw them outside the school gates, I had to make a run for it across the road. I got hit by a car as I tried to run away from them and was lucky not to be killed.'

Bullied children's stories

Sometimes something acts as a trigger for the bullying. That said, most bullies don't need any encouragement.

'We were playing another school for a netball trophy and I fluffed a shot and we lost. Since that day the other girls in the team have tormented me. They throw paint on my locker, spit in my face and steal my schoolbag. Once I tried to fight them and I ended up with a broken arm. I stopped going to school to escape them.' Carly (15)

'I didn't know that this guy was going out with a girl in my group when I said I liked him. His girlfriend was furious and since then she and her mates have made my life hell. None of them would talk to me and when I walk past them they try and trip me up. They sent me emails saying they're going to kill me.' Sally (14)

'My family come from Bangladesh and I can honestly say that I've never experienced racism. Then we moved to the UK and I started at a new school where I was the only Asian girl. The abuse started right away. They'd call me some awful things and tell me that I smelled 'like curry'. Eventually I left the school and although I'm at another one now where I'm the only Asian girl I don't have any problems and have lots of friends.' Shoba (16)

Bullies come in all shapes and sizes. It's not just other children who could be bullying your child. A teacher who seemed to take great delight from the fact that I had a speech impediment, which meant I couldn't pronounce my rs and is properly, used to pick on me. Guess who was always asked the solutions to the chemistry formulas where the answer was three? She'd get me to repeat it again and again until I was red in the face and felt like my head was going to explode. Thankfully the people in my class grew tired of it and she finally stopped. You see, bullies enjoy an audience. It adds to their sense of power.

Sometimes, bullies are not the people we expect. They may even be living under our own roofs.

Tip:
If you feel your child is being singled out by a teacher, contact the school. Ask your child to write down details of what happened and who was there at the time. Take that with you to the school when you go.

Case study

Tasha, 16, was bullied by her elder brother: 'He'd wait til my mum was out and order me around. If I didn't do what I was told he'd punch me. I was too scared to tell my mum.'

Inside the minds of the bullies

I asked children who'd ever bullied why they did it and was surprised by what they said:

- Bullies are often kids who have been bullied themselves. They like the sense of power they get when they turn the tables.

- They often have low self-esteem, like their victims.

- Bullying gives them confidence.

- Some admit to bullying to get attention.

- Some bullies admit that they can't stop.

- Some bullies come from abusive homes and say the only way that they know to interact and relate to others is through put downs and physical violence, as this is how they live at home.

- Many bullies started out as a friend of the child they targeted. This is very common.

Where does the bullying take place?

The common misconception is that bullying always happens at school, but those bullies are a crafty lot and are just as likely to do it outside school as much as in it. Danger areas can be anywhere. Your child's Saturday job, the library, in your own home whilst you're sitting watching the TV and your child's on the Internet, or even in a public place like a bus stop. Parents have to be alert and make sure they have the kind of friendly relationship with their child that means their child feels as though they can confide in them.

The effects of bullying

Bullying damages children, so it's no wonder that its effects are wide and ranging:

- **Drug taking and binge drinking** – Victims may drink or take drugs to blot out the pain to help them cope. Trying to get over traumatic events is one of the prime causes of drug and alcohol addiction.

- **Playing truant from school** – School is where the bad things happen. Is it any wonder bullied children don't want to go there? Would you?

- **Stress** – Being bullied is a stressful experience putting victims on edge all the time and making them jumpy. The stress of anticipating the next attack can be worse than the actual bullying itself.

- **Depression** – Many kids who are bullied end up having to be prescribed antidepressants. This is common, but is not a long-term solution to the problem. The only long-term solution is to get the bullying to stop.

- **Panic attacks** – Anxiety is what causes the tightness in the chest and shortness of breath that characterises panic attacks. Breathing exercises can help this. So too can blowing into a brown paper bag. The best cure though is to go right to the cause of the panic: the bullying itself.

- **Social phobias** – When a child is being bullied they may become terrified to go out and can become socially awkward. Years after I was bullied I developed agoraphobia. These days I find it difficult to go out alone without having panic attacks which make me feel like I'm dying.

- **Sleep disturbance** – Victims can suffer from nightmares and disturbing flashbacks. They may not be able to sleep at all or ask to sleep in your room.

- **Eating disorders** – In extreme cases, children develop eating disorders like bulimia or anorexia. They can't control their lives, so they try and control the one aspect that they believe they can – what they eat. Once an eating disorder gets a grip of your child, even if the bullying were to stop, the anorexia or bulimia won't simply go away. If you recognise your child here they need urgent medical help. Anorexia can kill; bulimia can permanently damage their internal organs and can cause kidney failure.

Tip:
We all live busy lives, but it's important to ask each other how our day went. This gives children a chance to tell you if there's anything troubling them.

- **Self-harming** – This can be difficult for parents to understand. Why would a child who is being harmed by bullies resort to harming themselves? Self-harmers claim to get a kind of 'release' from hurting themselves and harming themselves means they are in control. The most common method of self-harm is cutting, but it can also include doing things like burning with matches and cigarettes, sticking sharp objects into their arms and hitting their head off the wall.

- **Suicide** – In really extreme cases children can't take it anymore and decide to end their own lives. Most suicide attempts are cries for help, but some are genuine attempts to end their lives. The authors of *Bullycide; Death at Playtime*, a book, which looked at suicides caused by bullying, coined the term 'bullycide' to refer to children who killed themselves because of bullying.

Summing Up

Maybe you (thankfully) had little or no firsthand experience of bullying before you picked up this book, but now that you know more about bullying you will be more in tune with what's happening out there and able to help your child if they become a target. The question you'll be asking now will be – is my child being bullied?

The chances are that if you've picked up this book, the answer is yes. If that is the case, don't despair, there is a lot of help out there.

Let's turn to the next chapter for a run through of the signs that will help you to find out if your suspicions are indeed correct.

Is My Child Being Bullied?

As a parent, you are naturally protective towards your children and the thought that they are being bullied fills you with horror. The only thing that worries you more is the gnawing fear that they may be suffering in silence. If you think that your child is being bullied, how can you tell for sure? What are the signs to watch out for?

The good news is that there are many signs that any child is being bullied, but they are not always that easy to spot, so don't be too hard on yourself if you haven't noticed them til now. Many parents don't. Children can be very good at hiding things, which makes seeing them extremely difficult. Plus there's the fact that children can start to behave very strangely as they near adolescence through natural causes!

Signs to look out for:

- They turn up with ripped or missing clothes – This can be anything from a shirt that's torn to a scarf or jacket that's missing. Often kids will hide damaged clothes or dispose of them, so it may be a good idea to ask them about that sweatshirt they had on the other day that you can't find in the wash, or those jeans that look like they have paint on them.

- They don't want to go to school – You may even suspect that they've played truant or faked an illness to get out of going. Ask them about it. Say, 'Are you having problems at school and that's why you don't want to go?' Be gentle, not accusatory.

- They don't want to use the computer – Where once they were avid users of social networking sites like Facebook and Twitter, now they seem to be avoiding them altogether. Unfortunately, as well as giving them a chance to make new friends online and speak to old ones, there is also the possibility that the Internet can be used for nasty reasons.

- When their mobile phone says there's a new text they get jumpy and nervous – They could be getting sent nasty messages by a bully who may even be a former friend. They may not want to talk to a friend anymore. Is it just a simple falling out, or is there more? Gentle probing may get to the truth.

- They become sullen and uncommunicative – Okay, I know that could refer to most teenagers, but do they seem less willing to talk than usual? Do they tell you about their day, wait until you ask or snap at you when you do? Do they wait for you to ask and then grunt in reply or say nothing?

- They become withdrawn – They don't seem to like going out anymore and have few or no friends. They become extremely withdrawn, locking themselves away in their room and putting their music on so loud or plugging their iPod in so that they can't hear you. They may withdraw from doing family things such as going to the cinema or ten pin bowling; things they used to enjoy.

- Bruises and other signs of injury appear and there's no adequate explanation for – They may blame it on themselves saying they've been 'clumsy' or simply try to hide them. They may also come home with chewing gum or spit in their hair, or dog mess on their socks or shoes. Is the explanation they give plausible? Could it be a lie?

- They don't make eye contact when you talk to them – This may indicate that not all is well, or may perhaps just be down to the 'them and us' scenario that kids have towards adults, especially when they become teenagers.

- They stop being friends with someone and then get evasive when you ask about it – Former friends can become bullies. Friends can also fall out and drift apart. Which one is it, in this case?

- They're always speaking negatively about themselves – For example: calling themselves things like 'stupid' or 'useless' and never praising themselves or saying 'I'm good at that' or 'I can do that'. Have they always been so negative about themselves, or has something happened to make them feel that way?

- They stop arguing with their brothers or sisters – That's not typical sibling behaviour and may indicate that something is badly wrong. So too can not wanting to have anything to do with their brother or sister who they used to enjoy laughing and joking with.

- They've gone from being fiercely independent to always needing you there – They can't venture outside the home without you being with them. It's like they have this need to feel protected. Before when you accompanied them, they acted like they were embarrassed by you.

- They suffer from nightmares and panic attacks or general jumpiness – Young children may even start wetting the bed or suffering from nosebleeds.

- They become depressed and can't muster any enthusiasm for anyone or anything – They go off their food (including their favourite foods) and nothing you do to try and cheer them up will raise so much as a smile, including things that are usually guaranteed to bring a smile to their face, like buying them the computer game they were raving about or giving them the money to go and see the movie they've been talking about.

- They may be accused of bullying themselves – Many bullied kids start bullying others. This may include siblings or their own friends. Sometimes, those who have been bullied can be mistaken for bullies themselves when teachers see them standing up for themselves and misinterpret it as bullying. If this happens, listen to what your child has to say. Don't simply take the school's word for it. You will know if your child is lying.

- They start taking a different route to school to their usual route – Perhaps they get an earlier or later bus or walk home instead of getting the bus at all. They won't explain why, or they ask you to drive them to lessons every day and then return to pick them up.

- They change from being polite and well-mannered to being aggressive, rude or disobedient – This is something that has happened overnight and that can't simply be attributed to puberty. The reason they may be so angry is that they think you should notice they are being bullied or they are angry with themselves for 'allowing' themselves to be bullied. This is the way I felt.

- They stop doing something they enjoy like going swimming or doing out of school activities – Is it the activities they no longer want to do, or are they avoiding situations where they may come into contact with bullies?

- They become very secretive about their email and text messages and keep changing their passwords – Maybe they used to show you emails or cute pictures of puppies people sent them. But now they close their email the minute you are in the room. Is it them wanting their privacy or something more?

- You see them damaging their computer or mobile phone – Maybe it's a laptop or a mobile phone you caught them throwing across the room. Perhaps they're doing it because someone has upset them or so they can get a new one? Don't assume it's simple vandalism.

- They stop using their favourite Internet site or updating their blog – Where once they were on it all the time, now they tell you they hate it, even though you know it's dedicated to their favourite pop star or TV show. Are they bored with it or has someone left a nasty comment on their site? Bloggers can delete comments. They can also block certain people from leaving comments.

Why children hide bullying

As children get older they are less likely to confide in their parents. That fact and the very nature of bullying and how it makes the victim feel, combine to make many children feel that they can't tell on the bully. The telltale signs of bullying may be present and you may read them correctly, yet you may find that when you question your child about it you are met with complete silence or out and out denial.

This is because children hide the fact they are being bullied for a variety of reasons:

- **Shame** – Children are ashamed to admit that they are being bullied. They don't want to be seen as weak, or different, or to draw attention to themselves. All the bullied child wants is the bullying to stop. That's why a survey, conducted by Kidscape and sponsored by the National Lottery, concluded that many adults still bear the scars of being bullied because they never felt able to tell anyone. Of course it should be the bully who is ashamed, but that's seldom, if ever, the case. So the victim of bullying is left having to deal with not just the bullying, but also the shame that goes with it. I know, I've been there myself. Maybe you have too.

- **Denial** – Some kids can't believe what is happening to them. One minute they're minding their own business and the next, wham-bam, their life changes. They become someone who is being bullied and they feel as though they have been marked and nothing good will ever happen to them again. No wonder they enter a stage of denial, denying that they are being bullied, even sometimes laughing off the bullying as something that they can put up with when inside they are hurting.

- **They don't realise they are being bullied** – In some cases children may even be unsure that they are being bullied, something which sounds ridiculous, but you really have to experience bullying to be able to fully understand it. Bullied children often accuse themselves of being too sensitive or not being able to take a joke, because that's what they might hear someone else say.

- **Fear they won't be believed** – Well think about it. The way bullies operate is by trying to make sure they keep what they are doing a secret from the adults who can do something about it. Pupils aren't usually bullied inside the classroom in front of teachers: it's outside in the playground or outside the school gates where they are targeted, away from the watchful eye of adults who will intervene. Children think that if they can't prove what's happening – usually because they *can't* prove it – that they won't be believed.

- **Terror that the bullying won't stop** – 'If they (the bully) know that I've snitched they'll make it even worse for me,' is a common reason why the bullied child won't tell anyone about what's happening to them. They feel that if they do the abuse they're suffering will escalate.

- **They're worried they'll be treated like a grass** – What goes on in the world of your peers, stays there. That seems to be one of the codes by which young people live by. To break that code by getting adults involved in their world is often seen as a complete 'no-no'. Do that and you could find yourself being ostracised.

- **They don't want to bother you** – The self-esteem of bullied children can often be so low, because it's been eroded by the bullying, that they genuinely feel that they shouldn't be wasting anyone's valuable time because they're not worth it. Perhaps deep down they think that they must deserve what is happening to them because unless they did it wouldn't be happening. Or maybe it's a case of them thinking you are too busy to hear about it.

- **Your attitude** – You have to be realistic here and face facts – sometimes parents are not as approachable as they could be. One child I spoke to put up with a constant barrage of bullying for two years that included constant physical abuse after he heard his father say that he should stand up for himself more. As a result of that comment he never did tell his parents about the hell he was going through. Thankfully for him, they eventually found out and took the steps needed to get the harassment to stop, but in his situation careless words uttered by his father could have prevented the bullying from ever coming out into the open.

- **They've admitted defeat** – The bullying may have been going on so long that they just can't see any way or any day that it will ever come to an end. When children become this depressed it's vital that they get the urgent help that they need because they may be a suicide risk.

Tip:
Try and find at least an hour a week where you spend one-on-one time with your child. This can be watching a TV show together or playing a game of swing ball. This will help to build a good relationship with them that will make you seem more approachable.

What your child will say if they are being bullied to cover it up

Children can go to very great lengths to hide from adults the fact that they are being bullied. This may involve things like hiding ripped clothes and claiming that bruises came from normal everyday activities like playing football or larking about with their friends.

Here's a list of excuses that should set the alarm bells ringing straight away:

- 'I tore it playing football.' But they won't say who with.

- 'I lost/lent someone my lunch money.' But, they won't say who they lent it to or how they lost it.

- 'I dropped it and it broke.' Alarm bells should sound if they're usually careful with all their things.

- 'I got hit by the door/a football in PE. It was an accident.' Do they make eye contact when they tell you, or divert their gaze?

- 'I never liked that jacket so I gave it away.' Do they act all shifty when you ask them who they gave it to?

- 'I left my schoolbag on the bus.' Do they get upset when you suggest phoning the bus company to see if the bag's been handed in?

- 'I'm so clumsy. I'm always falling.' The person who said this had her arm broken by a bully who then took a photo of her writhing in agony on her mobile to circulate to all her friends.

- 'I swapped it with a kid at school.' Do they seem worried when you tell them to get whatever they swapped back?

Why children find it so hard to talk about bullying

We've discussed why children hide the fact they are being bullied chapter, but in order to fully understand why, who better to explain why they kept the bullying quiet than children and adults who were bullied.

'I felt like I was the dog poo someone had just stood on.' Clare (14)

'I started to believe that was just how things were. You got bullied or you bullied someone else.' Ryan (15)

'My parents were going through a bad divorce, the last thing they needed was my problems.' Tess (13)

'My mum's best friends with her (the bully) mum. I didn't think I'd be believed.' Sean (14)

'They threatened to hurt my little sister if I told on them.' Sophie (9)

Summing Up

When it comes to bullying the best advice is to:

- Trust your instincts.

- Discuss your worries openly and honestly with your child no matter how much you feel like you are clutching at straws. What's the worst thing that could happen – that you're wrong? Is that so terrible?

It isn't always easy to tell if your child is being bullied, when many children hide that fact. Most kids don't just come right out with it. For more in-depth advice about what to say to your child and how to make them stop blaming themselves for what's been happening to them, read the next chapter.

3

Talking to Your Child

You've already decided that your child is being bullied and the question now is how do you get them to open up about it so you can get the bullying to stop?

Getting bullied children to open up is a difficult process. They may have bottled it up for so long that they find it difficult to talk about it not necessarily because they don't want to, but perhaps they have difficulty articulating what's been happening. Maybe they feel scared to tell you because they worry about how you'll react. Perhaps they just don't 'want to be any trouble?'

Bullies often threaten to hurt people close to their victims. In one shocking case I encountered, bullies threatened to kill a 13-year-old girl's beloved dog.

Getting your child to open up

If you want your child to feel able to talk to you, there are certain things you should say and ones you should avoid.

Dos:

- Be prepared. Know what you are going to say. The first words you utter when you talk to your child are critical. Make them the right ones.

- Use the Internet to look at information on bullying because it's an invaluable source of free information.

- Pick a place where there are no interruptions. The best way to talk to your child is one-on-one. If they are other people around it will only make them self-conscious.

- Stress that what is happening to them is not their fault. The bullied usually think it is.

- Ensure they know that you will do everything that you can to get the bullying to stop.

- Get specific details from them about what's been happening. Did anyone witness any of these events? How did what happen make them feel? Who was involved?

- Discuss with them what action you can take. They have to know that the decision is a joint one. Give them some of the power they have lost to the bully or bullies back. Ask them what they want you to do before deciding on a course of action such as contacting the school or speaking to the bully or bullies' parents. Bullied children need to know that something will be done.

- Tell them if you were bullied or anyone you know was, so that they can see that you empathise with them and have an understanding of what it's like to be their age and have their problems.

- Be sensitive when asking them questions so that it doesn't come across as an interrogation or that you don't really believe them.

Don'ts:

- It's not easy, but do *not* get angry. The bully isn't in the room, but your child is, and if you get angry they'll think you're angry with them and not the bully.

'You've already decided that your child is being bullied and the question now is how do you get them to open up about it so you can get the bullying to stop?'

- Never suggest that it may be their fault. When 15-year-old Mary Jane told her mum about the bullying her mum responded with, 'What did you do to cause that?' The blame for bullying has to be placed firmly at the bully's door because it is never the victim's fault.

- Don't tell them to stand up for themselves and ask why they didn't. It makes it sound like you are blaming them. Besides, maybe they did try to stand up for themselves and it backfired, making them feel worse; or perhaps that's just not the kind of thing they can do because you brought them up to be a decent, compassionate human being who respects others.

- Refrain from telling everyone about the bullying or you will make your child feel like everybody knows and is talking about him or her.

- Don't be angry with them because the bullying has been going on for so long and they haven't told you. This is a natural reaction not because you are angry with them, but because deep down you are angry with yourself.

- Don't threaten the bullies or their parents with violence. That's the last thing you should do. Of course you're angry, but violence never solved anything. Suggesting it does may make your child feel like the bullying is their fault for not punching the bully on the nose.

- Don't make promises that you can't keep i.e. say you'll take them out of school if need be and teach them at home when you have no intention of doing that. Don't destroy their trust in you.

- On no account should you promise to keep what your child has told you confidential. This can be difficult for a parent to do, especially when your child is so obviously upset, but there's no way you can take action if you keep what they have told you to yourself.

- Whatever you do, do not be tempted to take your child out of school and take them away on holiday to give them a break. The bullying problem has to be sorted out now as a matter of great urgency. Leave it until later and your child will only worry.

Tip: Choose somewhere they are comfortable to talk. This can be in their room or on the seafront eating ice cream cones.

The right questions to ask

You've ascertained that the bullying is going on, but what do you need to know now?

- How long has this been going on?

- Who was involved?

- Can they name names?

- What exactly has been happening? Does the bullying involve things like physical violence or theft of property – criminal offences? This may come in useful if you need to go to the police.

- Were there any witnesses, or was it caught on CCTV?

- Did they tell anyone? This can include anyone from friends to teachers.

- Have they got any records of the bullying? For instance, did they write about it in their diary or in an email/text message to a friend? A heart-rending record of the bullying can come in handy when it comes to approaching the school.

- If the bullying happened online, keep copies of the offending emails or messages. Print them out if you can. Take a screen grab of any evidence. If they were bullied by text message, get your child to keep a copy in their inbox. Ask them to send it to you, so you have one too.

- Do they have any injuries now? Perhaps they need medical help. If they do have injuries, take them to the doctors (so they have a record) and take photographs of them. Ask your child exactly how they got them. Documenting evidence in this way will come in useful later.

- Do they feel able to talk to a teacher about the torment they've suffered? Many children have a favourite teacher. Having a teacher whose aware of what's gone on will help you when it comes to approaching the school about the bullying.

Tip:
Have any of your family or friends had to cope with bullying? If so, ask them for advice on what they did.

Getting your child to open up

In view of all the things we've discussed, talking to your child about bullying may not be that easy. You need to pick your moment and your approach carefully. Here are some suggested scenarios for you to try:

Scenario 1 – Have a general 'we're here for you' talk

Children need to be reminded that they are loved. Take this as an opportunity to ask them if anything is troubling them. Some children never tell about bullying because they just don't know how to pick the time to tell you.

Scenario 2 – Bring up a particular incident

Sometimes it's best not to pussyfoot around the issue and to actually come out and ask them if their shirt was torn by someone at school/or someone broke their phone. Don't do this when they are distracted by the TV or are listening to music. Don't do it in front of their siblings. The best place to do this is probably in their bedroom or in the garden where you won't be disturbed and can have a real heart-to-heart. Admit that you are worried that they may be getting bullied at school and try and gauge their reaction to see if it confirms it, even if their words don't.

Tip:
Suggest that if they are worried about anything they can write you a letter. Sometimes it can be easier to write it down.

Scenario 3 – The day out in a relaxed atmosphere

A change of scenery can work wonders. Try taking your child out somewhere you know that they will enjoy. This can be anywhere. For younger children, try an amusement park or a trip to the beach. For older kids, go for a concert with their favourite band, if it's your daughter take her to get her hair done and if it's your son take him to get his favourite football team's top. Taking them out of their home environment will allow them to relax, making them more liable to open up to you about what's been happening.

Scenario 4 – Ask someone else to talk to your child

There are times when parents have to step aside and enlist other people's help and this may be the occasion for that. If you are worried that they won't be able to open up to you about the bullying then ask someone who is close to them to speak to them. This can be their grandmother, auntie, big sister or elder brother, or friend – a responsible person who they relate well to. What's important is that your child admits they are being bullied not who it is they tell.

Glued Mouth Syndrome

There is a strong chance that, despite your best efforts, you won't be able to get them to speak to you. You can't force them to admit to what's been happening, so if your initial attempt to get it out of your child fails, try and try again. Admitting you're being bullied isn't easy. It takes a lot of courage.

What your child is likely to say

Your child may try and play down the bullying. They may blame themselves or claim that it's stopped. That's typical of the way bullied children behave.

They are also likely to have questions for you that you will need to answer the best you can. They need that reassurance.

Here are some of the most likely questions they will ask. It may be useful to think about how you will answer them *before* you speak to your child:

'Did you know, for example, that movie star Tom Cruise was bullied because he was dyslexic and was a 'weedy kid'?'

- Why me? – This is one of the most common questions that the bullied child asks. The child needs to know that the bullying has nothing to do with them personally.

- Why do bullies do it? – They need to understand why people can be so cruel.

- Did I do something to deserve it? – They feel like they've brought it upon themselves in some way. This is your opportunity to tell them that's not true.

- Can you get it to stop? – They need reassurance from you that the bullying will stop.

- Is this happening because no one likes me?

- Will I always feel as bad as this? – Be positive about the bullying finally stopping. Tell them that once the bullying ends they will return to their happy old self. Talk about something good that's happening in the future like a holiday or family party.

- Were you bullied? – A little white lie may not go amiss here. Sometimes parents have to do that so that their children can feel you understand them.

He was bullied too you know!

Knowing that stars were bullied too and still managed to come out the other side and be a success, can make those who've been bullied feel better about themselves and what has happened to them. Dropping their names into the conversation when talking about bullying with your child can make them more likely to admit they've been bullied if they know that celebrities have suffered too.

- Did you know, for example, that movie star Tom Cruise was bullied because he was dyslexic and was a 'weedy kid'?

- Kate Middleton was also bullied. She's shown the bullies and is now a princess.

- David Beckham was also targeted at school and claims he was the last one to be picked for the school football team.

- Beautiful actress Michelle Pfeiffer, was teased about her looks, especially her lips, and was nicknamed 'Michelle Mudturtle' by schoolmates. She used to run home crying.

- Angelina Jolie went through a hard time when she was bullied at school.

- Oscar-nominated Hollywood actress Samantha Morton was in and out of care homes when she was a child and was mercilessly bullied by other children. She once found broken glass and excrement in her bed and a teddy bear and diary her mother had given her were burnt.

Tip:
The more celebrity names you mention the better. Make your child realise they can have a happy and successful life – after the bullying. Reassure them that they are not alone.

Summing Up

Finding out your child is being bullied is a very distressing and difficult time. First and foremost they need to know that it is not their fault. Too many bullied kids blame themselves.

It's imperative that they are also aware that you will do everything you can to get the bullying to stop.

After discussing the bullying with you, your child will no longer feel alone.

4

Why My Child?

Discovering that your child is being bullied can be difficult for a parent to come to terms with. Why is it happening to my child? Am I to blame? Did I not raise them right? Are my parenting skills at the root of what's been happening? You will ask yourself these questions and more as you try to make sense of it all.

It's only natural that you should feel that way. No matter how grown up and independent children get, you may still think of them as your babies and believe that you should be able to protect them from anything. It's a hard blow for any parent to take when they realise that they can't.

Ultimately no parent can protect their child from all the bad things in the world, including bullies, but that doesn't stop them from feeling that they should be able to.

So, why the blame game?

Am I to blame?

In the case of bullying, parents may fear that they have done something to make their children a target for bullies. Perhaps you feel you haven't equipped them with the necessary social skills? Maybe you feel you didn't give them the toughness that they need to cope with difficult situations and people. Terrible parent that you are; bringing up your kids to be decent, compassionate human beings instead of insensitive morons.

Not that it's any consolation, but your child will be blaming themselves too, because ultimately the main problem with bullying is that everyone blames themselves for it except for the ones causing all the trouble – the bullies.

Tip:
If you find yourself blaming yourself for the bullying, write down the reasons why. Now read it back as though someone else wrote it. Does any of it make sense?

Why your child being bullied isn't your fault

One of the most common myths of all about bullying is that it's the fault of parents who have made their kids targets. Perhaps the parent was bullied themselves and fears that they have passed on a bullying gene or a mode of behaviour that makes their offspring behave in a certain way that attracts bullying. Maybe it's because they haven't bought their kid the same kind of fancy trainers that everyone else is wearing. Or it could even be that their child has been brought up to be gentle and kind and not tough.

The truth is of course is that the only person to blame is the bully themselves and any adult who knowingly allows them to carry on with their behaviour.

Shattering the myths about bullying

It's easy to be sucked into the myths that surround bullying and to treat them as fact. In order to understand the nature of the beast we are dealing with here, we have to examine them and the rationale behind them. Then smash them to smithereens:

'My child must have done something that triggered the bullying.'

The reasoning: Nothing happens without a good reason. This rationale suits the bullies because it exonerates them of all blame. It's not their fault. It's the children they pick on.

False

If someone gets mugged you don't turn round and say they deserved it, it's the way they dangled their purse about, dared to wear that gold necklace, or thought that they could have that £400 mobile phone. Bullying is a crime and the victims are never to be blamed. Doing that just falls into the bullies' hands.

'Bullying is just part of growing up.'

The reasoning: Everybody gets bullied. It just happens. Bad things do.

False

That may be a sad reality for many children but that doesn't make it right or acceptable. Every child has a right to live in a nurturing environment without fear where they can enjoy their childhood and grow into well-rounded adults.

Bullying forces kids to live in fear and can ruin their potential as well as changing their character irrevocably. How is any of that in any way natural and normal? Childhood is meant to be a carefree time free of worry and not a fearful one.

'Bullying toughens kids up.'

The reasoning: This myth seems to imply that it's an important part of a child's development to be bullied. That children need to encounter and face up to the bullies of this world so that they will be tough enough to know how to deal with them when they are adults.

False

There's overwhelming evidence to suggest that bullying weakens people instead of toughening them up. Why else would adults still speak with terror of the bullying they suffered when they were at school? The bullying has had such a profound and often devastating effect on them that the effects still linger even long after the bullying has stopped.

I know that from my own bitter experience. Even today I can't pass a gang of teenage boys without breaking out into a cold sweat, because it was a group like that who terrorised me when I was at school. I know this seems illogical and an overreaction, but that is genuinely how I feel.

'The bullying is my fault because I'm never there.'

The reasoning: It's the kids of negligent parents who get bullied.

False

These days a heap of blame seem to get dumped at the doors of parents who have to work to ensure their kids are fed and clothed, so why shouldn't it be the case with bullying?

Kids from all kinds of families get bullied. You could be a stay at home parent, the kind who makes their kid a packed lunch and sees them off to school every day and your son or daughter may still end up getting bullied. Being bullied has nothing to do with whether you are there for your kid 24 hours a day or only spend a couple of hours with them if you are lucky. Single parent families, families where both parents work – bullies don't discriminate. Besides, no parent can be with their child every minute of every day, which is what you would have to do to ensure they don't get bullied.

Tip:
Any clichés people trot out are usually myths.

'Bullying is something that has always gone on, that will always go on, and there's nothing we can do about it.'

The reasoning: Things don't change.

False

This is the kind of defeatist attitude that allows bullying to thrive. Instead of trying to stop it, people just shrug their shoulders and say, 'There's nothing we can do'. If everybody did that what would happen? Bullies would just be left to get on with it and their victims left to suffer, usually in silence. Is that what people want? I think we all know that it's not.

Bad things happen because people stand by and do nothing. Who wants to be one of those people?

The apathetic attitude to bullying could just as well be applied to say global warming. Why bother trying to stop it? We want to try because although we face an uphill struggle it's human nature to want to right wrongs: to change things. It's what makes us marvellous human beings instead of robots who merely accept things.

Just remember that if every person does their bit to stop bullying it will eventually become one of those awful things that happened in the past, like children being sent to work houses in Victorian times or up chimneys, that people talk about in hushed tones, disgusted that it ever happened in the first place.

'If my child just stood up to the bully the bullying would stop.'

The reasoning: Bullies are looking for a sign of weakness and when they find it that's when they latch on to their prey. By that same rationale if a man gets mugged in the street by two assailants it would be his fault not his attackers. Well, he should have told the muggers to take a hike surely?

False

Often this is the stuff of folklore. Not all bullies back down when challenged because the very nature of bullying means that quite often bullies surround themselves with their friends who are often bullies too. This means that a child could easily find themselves outnumbered. Bullying isn't always one-on-one; it's usually the cowardly bully, their mates and the victim, who is often alone.

'If my kid punched the bully on the nose that would be the perfect solution.'

The reasoning: The bully is looking for weakness. Punch him on the nose and he will realise your child isn't weak and leave them alone.

False

Maybe it would work if the bullying was on a one-to-one basis, but violence is not the answer to anything. What kind of message does it is send out to kids when anyone suggests that it is? Inevitably all violence leads to more violence.

In one case I found through my research, Alistair* was threatened with a shovel by the teenager who had been bullying him for months. He grabbed the shovel from him and in the tussle ended up knocking him flying. Guess who ended up being cautioned by the police?

Assault is a crime and bullies are often the type of people who will be perfectly happy to bully a smaller child, but if they happened to get hurt they would be pretty quick to get the police involved. Do you want your child to have a criminal record when it's the bully who should have one?

*Name has been changed.

'I have raised a weak child because only weak people get bullied.'

The reasoning: Bullies only pick on those they see as weak.

False

Terrible parent that you are, you have raised a child who respects others and doesn't bully other kids. Research shows that they are the children most likely to get bullied. How can you look in the mirror?

The stark fact is that kids are bullied for all sorts of reasons. Maybe it's the colour of their skin, their weight (too skinny or overweight), their religion, them not wearing 'the right trainers' or the fact that they are popular/smart/beautiful/funny/have a Roman nose. Whatever it is, remember it's merely an excuse for the bully who will use any reason to bully someone.

'This is my fault because I was bullied at school too.'

The reasoning: I have turned my child into a miniature version of me, a victim.

False

It's understandable that discovering that the same terrible, damaging thing that happened to you is also happening to your child will bring back painful memories and feelings that you would rather forget. That doesn't mean that you are correct when you blame yourself for the bullying. Most children will encounter bullying at some stage.

'I was bullied at school too and it never did me any harm, so my child's just being oversensitive.'

The reasoning: This happened to me. I got over it.

Tip: Self-defence classes offer the ideal opportunity to teach your child how to defend themselves.

False

Have you ever heard the phrase 'different strokes for different folks'? People react to bullying differently and there are different degrees of bullying. Besides, the bullying that goes on now may be different to what you suffered. There's much evidence to suggest that nowadays bullies are more prone to using physical violence and the everyday use of mobile phones and the Internet means that they have new ways of tormenting their victims. It is far easier for bullies to reach their victims wherever they are.

Until you are in someone's shoes, including your own child's, it's impossible for you to know how the bullying makes them feel, and how severe it actually is.

'If I move my child to another school that will definitely solve the problem.'

The reasoning: I can make the problem go away by changing schools.

False

Yes this could work, but what happens if your child is targeted again at their new school? What then? Do you move them to another school and one after that? As difficult as it may be, bullying has to be dealt with, not swept under the carpet.

As well as dealing with the bullying you also have to try and counteract the effects on your child's self-esteem. Chapter 9 will offer ways to help you to do that.

Summing Up

You find out that your child is being bullied and you ask your friends if it's happened to their children and they say no. You have a right to ask yourself why is it happening to your child? Who wouldn't ask that question?

The simple fact is that what's happening is not your fault or your child's. Don't believe the myths that say otherwise.

5

How To Prevent Your Child Getting Bullied

'Bullying is just a fact of life and nothing can be done about it.'

'Bullying will always go on.'

'Children are either bullies or they're bullied.'

Sadly, there are people who genuinely believe those statements to be true. But they're wrong. There are steps that you and your child can take to lessen their chance of getting bullied. And, the good news is, that they can be used in conjunction with other roads parents go down to stop bullying, including going to your child's school if they are being picked on. Let's call it bully avoidance.

Who is the bully?

Before we try and adopt some bully avoidance strategies, we first have to know what we are dealing with here. We have to build a profile of the bully.

Who are they and who are they most likely to pick on? How do they operate? And most importantly, how can that help you to keep your child free of harm?

Not every bully is the same but they tend to share the same characteristics:

- Bullies pick on children who are different; often it is these very qualities that make some children susceptible to bullies that are also the ones that make them special. Bullies can be jealous of their victims for being good at certain sports, academically gifted or attractive.

- Bullies pick on children who lack confidence. A child who walks about looking down at their feet is more likely to be bullied that one who walks with their head held high. Bullies are repelled by confidence.

- Bullies usually pick on children who are on their own because they are cowards. If they thought that the tables could be turned on them they wouldn't bully anyone.

- Bullies tend to do it in groups usually of friends or other victims because they like an audience. This also gives them back-up and strength of numbers. Bullies only bully when they know that they can get away with it because no one who witnesses what is happening will speak up.

- Bullies are usually physically stronger than the person they are bullying and are often older. They don't want to take the chance of someone they're taunting belting them one. This is usually why parents urging their child to 'just hit him/her back' just isn't an option. Violence never should be.

- They have a distinct lack of sympathy for their victim and can't put themselves in their shoes or anyone else's for that matter. They often have trouble relating to anyone else.

- Many bullies come from homes where violence is used as a means to get what they want. Bullying can be a learned behaviour, which means that it can also be unlearned.

What you can do to prevent your child from being bullied

As parents there are things that you can do to help your children, especially now you know how most bullies operate. These methods won't completely rule out the chance of your child being bullied, but what they will do is greatly cut down the opportunities for the bullying to take place.

Strategy 1 – Encourage your child to be themselves

True, being an individual can lead to children being singled out because they are different, but it will give them the confidence that repels bullies, not attracts them.

Achieving this:

- Don't automatically buy them things that other kids their age are getting. Young people are all different and may want different things. Ask them what they would like. What they want. Let them develop their own likes and dislikes. And if they take up an unusual hobby encourage them. Take an active interest. Let them be their own person and to feel good about being that person.

Strategy 2 – Encourage your child to socialise

No child deserves to be bullied, but there are certain character traits that make some children more susceptible to bullying. The main one is social awkwardness. Other children may pick up on this and that's when the trouble can start. That's why it's important that children make friends. New friends can give children, especially ones who've been bullied, a new lease of life.

Achieving this:

- Try inviting some of their friends around and make them know that they are always welcome.

- Within reason, allow your child to accept invitations to socialise with their friends.

- If your friends have kids encourage them to socialise with yours.

- Encourage your child to participate in physical activities, even if they are reluctant. Physical exercise is good for a child's confidence and there's always at least one sport that even a non-sporty child can enjoy. They don't have to be good at it. It's all about having fun.

Tip:
Point out to your child that being called a bully is an insult.

Strategy 3 – Have your very own bully drill

If your child feels that they are in a situation that they can't handle, they are being chased by bullies for example, decide on a safe place that they can go to like a shop or a neighbour's house. This will give them a safety net and stop them feeling the loneliness that many bullied children feel because they have no one to turn to at the very point where they need it most.

Achieving this:

- Discuss this with them beforehand (try and be light-hearted about it, not alarmist) and give them a number of an available adult they can call to come and get them.

Strategy 4 – Raise an independent child

It's difficult in this day and age for parents to feel safe about letting their children out of their sight, but they've got to learn to fly sometime. Having an independent child means having a confident child and that will make them less likely to be bullied.

Achieving this:

- If they are old enough, let them go places with their friends that they usually go with you, say into town or to the bowling alley.

- If you pick them up from school then let them take the bus for a change and give them money to go for some food with their friends.

- Give them some responsibility. This will show that you have faith in them and trust them. This can be anything from letting them walk the pet dog, to choosing what you're all having for dinner.

Strategy 5 – Ensure your child knows how to report incidents of bullying

One teacher I spoke to about bullying, said that the reason it's such a big problem is that often the victims aren't very coherent or detailed when it comes to telling adults about what's happened to them. Every incident of bullying has to be reported as succinctly as possible in order for something to be done about it.

Achieving this:

Tip:
Always make sure your child has enough money in their mobile phone to call home. Put alternative numbers in they can phone in case the home number is engaged.

- Teach your child that any report of bullying should include: What happened? Where and when did this happen? Who did what? Who else saw what happened? What they did. How what happened made them feel.

Strategy 6 – Educate your child about bullying and bullies

I know from my own bitter experience that when you are being bullied you are caught in a vicious circle of doubt and you believe that you have done something to merit what is happening to you. What you need is for someone to say that what's happened is not your fault and that it won't go on forever.

Achieving this:

- Tell them that bullying is never the victim's fault; it's the bully who is in the wrong and that if you found out they were being bullied you would never blame them.

- Make sure they know that you regard bullies as cowards and they are the ones who should be ashamed, not the people they pick on.

- Stress that bullying can be stopped.

- Assure them that you will do everything that you can to stop them from being bullied, including taking them out of school if necessary, but only if you really mean it.

Tip:
Buy your child a fancy notebook or diary they can write in.

Strategy 7 – Make sure that your child knows the importance of body language

There's something that I call the 'victim' stance. It's when your shoulders are hunched, your mouth is unsmiling, your head is down and you avoid making any eye contact. Bullies love this stance. You want your child to walk in a confident manner even if they don't feel confident.

Achieving this:

- Teach them some confident body language. Get them to practise in front of a mirror.

- If this doesn't do the trick, try sending them to an Alexander Technique teacher. Actors go to these specialists who teach people how to achieve the right posture.

Strategy 8 – Make sure that your child has a safe and nurturing environment at home

This will help give them more confidence and also make them feel more able to tell you if they are being bullied.

The confidence that bullies have is derived mainly from the fact that in most cases they know that their victim won't tell. By creating a home life where your child feels that they can tell you anything, you shift the power balance in your child's favour.

Achieving this:

- Talk with your child, not at them or down to them. This way they are more likely to come to you when they have a problem.

- Try and stay calm at all times and don't raise your voice. No one gets their point across by shouting, but everyone does it.

- If you have a problem discuss it with them calmly, don't shout.

- Be interested in your child and their life. Ask them what they did in school that day. Spend time with them, even if it's only to watch a TV programme. Ask them what they think about the shows they're watching and the computer games they're playing.

- If they do something well, tell them. Children need praise to feel good about themselves.

Tip:
Acting classes are a good idea and will teach them about posture and behaviour.

Strategy 8 – Make sure they know how to keep safe online

Cyberbullying is a major problem and the reason many parents now monitor the sites their kids visit.

Achieving this:

- Make sure your child knows the importance of *never* giving their password or user details to anyone for any of their online accounts, including email and social networking sites. Someone could use that and cause mischief, including making it look like your child has been posting nasty messages about someone else.

- Make sure your child never posts their address or says where they live. There have been countless stories over the years of crowds turning up to private birthday parties at young people's homes simply because users on sites like Facebook have posted personal info.

- Teach them how to use the 'report' button on sites. Some sites also have an 'ignore' function where users can block comments from people.

- Make sure they know about the 'block' function on sites like Twitter and Facebook. Using this, they can block other users from viewing their page or sending them messages.

- Explain the danger of following or adding someone to their friends that they don't know. Bullies can be people they've only met in cyberspace.

- If someone gets into your child's account on one of their sites, they should close down that account and open a new one with new passwords.

- Make sure your child knows that any pictures or details they post online will be viewed by other people – even ones they don't know – unless the site has a 'privacy' or 'show only to friends' option.

- Drum it into your child that they should *never* meet anyone they've met online.

- Remember, as a last resort, you may be able to block certain websites from your computers at home. Ask your Internet provider for details.

Tip:
Doing some role play where one of you plays the bully may help.

Help and advice

The most popular social networking site in the UK, Facebook, has a 'family safety centre' with details of their privacy settings, advice for parents and teens. Go to www.facebook.com/safety

One of Facebook's executives has also posted a video on the site advising users on how to bully-proof themselves on the site. You can view it by going to http://www.facebook.com/video/video.php?v=320030310522

The second most popular social networking site in the UK, Twitter, also has a 'help centre'. You can report violations (like bullying) and compromised accounts. Go to http://support.twitter.com

For more information on cyberbullying go to www.stopcyberbullying.org/index2.html

There's also advice on the Direct Gov site. Go to http://www.direct.gov.uk and type 'keeping children safe online' into the search engine for some more general advice.

What your child can do

No child can completely bully-proof their life unless they stay in all day and hide under the duvet, but there are things that children can do to limit their chances of being bullied.

Children should:

**Tip:
Don't forget that email addresses can be blocked. If your child starts to get vindictive emails from one address, they don't have to suffer.**

- Never give out their phone number to anyone except their closest friends. Text bullying is a new trend.

- Try and be with a group of friends at all times. Bullies tend to hang about in gangs and pick on children on their own. They're too cowardly to target whole groups of people because there's a chance that they will be the ones made to look stupid.

- Leave classes with friends or with a teacher. This is especially pertinent if your child has been the target of bullies in the past.

- Avoid places where bullies are likely to be.

- Never take expensive things to school. Jealously may attract bullies.

- Ask bullies to repeat what they've just said (bullies hate this). Some victims of bullying say that it helps if they have replies ready to regular taunts because the bully isn't expecting it.

- Try to act more confident – even if they don't feel it.

What if my child is the bully?

Not every child who is involved in bullying is on the receiving end. This may come as a shock to parents when they discover their own child is a bully.

How to stop your child bullying:

- Try and get to the root of why they do it. Were they bullied themselves and they think that by bullying others they will get back the power that they lost? Have they learnt this behaviour in the home? Maybe you should be looking at how you behave. Do you adopt bullying behaviour? Be honest. Often bullies learn the behaviour from family members. If the behaviour is uncharacteristic, could something be worrying them and that's why they are lashing out?

- Make sure that they know how much you disapprove of their behaviour, but don't say that you're so ashamed of them, or that you're disowning them, even if you feel that way. They've got to know that it's their behaviour you disapprove of, not them. They need an incentive to change.

- Work out a way for them to stop bullying. Maybe they think that aggression is the best way to deal with any kind of conflict. Teach them other ways.

- Come up with a suitable way that they can make amends for the bullying. This could be something as simple as apologising to their victim or writing an essay to be read out in front of the class.

- Look at how they resolve conflicts within the home. This can give you a clue as to how they behave when they're away from your scrutiny.

- Get them to empathise with their victim. Bullies tend to lack empathy and this is why they continue to bully. Try role-playing where you give them a taste of what it's like to be on the receiving end for a change.

Tip:
If in doubt about how to keep your child safe online, use the Internet to find out more information. Put search terms like 'staying safe on Facebook' and 'how to beat cyberbullying' and you'll find a wealth of info. Make it fun by having a race to see who can come up with the best advice.

Summing Up

- Bullying doesn't have to be a fact of life.

- To prevent your kids from being bullied you have to be aware of how the bully behaves and come up with strategies to counteract that.

- There are things that our children can do to prevent becoming victims, like ensuring they are always with friends, never giving out their phone number and being confident.

- Bullying may be a problem for your child in a different way to the way you might think. They might be the one doing the bullying.

6

Going to the School

Y ou find out that your child is being bullied at school and, all guns blazing, you want to march right down there and give them what for. A perfectly natural reaction, but how many parents do you think have done that and come away feeling that they've been brushed aside or feeling foolish because they haven't gone to the school with the facts that they need to get something done? Too many unfortunately.

Before you even think about going to the school you need to be prepared: to know you and your child's rights inside out. Go armed with the necessary information at your disposal and you have more chance of the school taking the necessary action to stop the bullying dead in its tracks. Don't go prepared and you face making it a long drawn out process that will infuriate you and cause further damage to the injured party – your child.

Why the school should be your first port of call

As parents are legally obligated to send their children to school or to educate them at home, schools are regarded as being in loco parentis*. Whilst your child is at school they are effectively the ones who are deputising for you the absent parent. Schools have a duty of care to your child and are obligated to provide children with a safe learning environment. Bullying infringes upon that duty.

In addition, by law schools must have a policy on bullying, which clearly states their responsibilities and the sanctions they will take to deal with bullying if and when it arises.

*This fact was established by the Court of Appeal who decreed that the school head teacher stands in loco parentis (in place of the parents).

Tip:
Most schools will still be concerned about bullying that goes on outside their gates, even if they are not currently legally obliged to be.

What schools aren't responsible for

Before you go to the school all pumped up demanding to know what they are going to do about little Ryan or Sarah being bullied, there are a two things that you need to know.

Fact 1 – Schools are not deemed to be responsible for bullying that goes on outside the school gates

This was the surprise High Court ruling in 1990 in a case brought by Leah Bradford-Smart who claimed she'd suffered 'persistent and prolonged bullying' for three years and sought damages in court. Her lawyer argued that the school still had a duty of care to pupils outside the gates, but the judge decided otherwise.

In most cases this verdict won't harm your case against the bully because in the majority of incidences the actual harassment is likely to happen within the school grounds at least at some point.

If your child is being bullied on the bus, please refer to the section in the next chapter which covers exactly that.

Fact 2 – A school is not treated as being negligent when it comes to bullying if they are unaware that the bullying was taking place

They have to be made aware of it first or it has to be obvious that bullying is taking place i.e. incidents were witnessed by teachers. This is only fair when you think about it. How can you be responsible for your child being victimised if you were unaware that it was happening? The answer is that you can't be and nor should you be. In the interest of fairness the same even-handedness has to be applied to schools.

From the moment they are made aware of it, and have been given enough time to act, they are liable.

The difference between primary school V secondary school bullying

If your child is being bullied at primary it's best if you approach their class teacher initially. As someone who works with your child on a daily basis, they will be the ones in the best position to sort out any problems between pupils. If you are not satisfied with their response then go to the head teacher or the deputy head.

For secondary school bullying arranging a meeting with your child's guidance teacher or the head teacher or his or her deputy is best.

Equipping yourself with the facts

Before you approach the school it's best to be prepared. You will need:

- A copy of your school's anti-bullying policy. The school have to provide this to any parent who asks by law, so phone up the school secretary and ask for a copy. Having it to hand will ensure you know exactly how the school has said it will act in the circumstances and you can demand that they follow it to the letter. Many schools have their policy printed on their website too.

Tip:
It's always best to phone the school and ask them for the name of the person you should contact.

- Remember the burden of proof is on you to prove that the bullying is taking place. Get details of the harassment that's taken place. Where and when did it happen? Who were the perpetrators/witnesses? Does your child have any proof, like bruises or torn clothes? Be exact about everything and take notes. There's no point in saying that your son had his head shoved down the toilet once and not being able to specify when this happened. If your child has written down details this can be useful, as can emails they have sent to friends about what's been happening.

- Have exact details of how this has affected your child. Have they developed a terror of going to school/started wetting the bed? Have their grades gone down dramatically? Have they received medical attention? One mother I spoke to had to give her son something to help him sleep when he developed insomnia. Details like these that illicit action from schools.

Tip:
You may feel like suggesting that the bully deserves a slap (which is understandable because you're angry), but don't say that to the school as they may accuse you of being aggressive.

What action can the school take?

There is a raft of measures that schools can take. These include:

- Increasing supervision in areas where bullies are most likely to strike. Some schools may agree to put teachers on school buses to supervise pupils.

- Supervising the bully.

- Speaking to the bully and their parents. This will most likely happen after a letter has been sent out to his or her parents requesting their son/daughter's presence at the school.

- Issuing a full warning to the bully. This will include details of any action that will be taken if the harassment of a fellow pupil doesn't cease.

- Some schools have schemes whereby the bully is asked to explain their actions to their victim with an adult present. Being made to face up to what they're doing may shame them into stopping.

- Detention.

- Internal exclusion within school. Say your son is being bullied and he's on the football team, the bully could face being unable to play on the team unless he modifies his behaviour.

- Suspension from school for a set period.

- The bully may be referred to a child psychologist.
- Being expelled. This will only be used as a last resort and in extreme cases.

The ins and outs of your meeting at the school

You've made that appointment and now it's time to get down to the nitty-gritty.

Should I take my child with me?

It depends on the child. How do they feel about it? If they feel awkward about being there then don't force them to be as they've suffered enough. You can always get them to write a letter about what's been happening and how it's making them feel.

Should I take someone with me?

Two heads are better than one. Both parents should be there if possible. If that is impossible then have a suitable adult deputise for the missing parent. Have a witness to the proceedings.

What proof do I need?

Bring any evidence you have i.e. a doctor's note or a schoolbook that the bullies have defaced. Showing the school bruises your child has or a ruined piece of clothing can be very effective. Also, show copies of offending emails, web posts and text messages.

Can I ask for more supervision for my child or the bully?

If bullying is happening in the changing rooms, in the corridors or playground then ask for supervision to be increased. If the school says it does not have the resources then explain that you are not expecting every child to receive increased supervision, only the bully. The school may still object to this, but you can always ask.

Tip:
If your child wants to attend the meeting it may be best to speak to the school and get your child some time off school. That way they won't have to be excused from class in front of the bullies if they are classmates of theirs.

Should I take notes of what is said?

Yes do. You may be too stressed at the time to fully take in what is being said, which is why notes are essential. You can look back on them later.

How can I make sure the school do as they've promised?

Make sure you know exactly what action they have promised to take. Get a timeline. When will they do as they've promised? Get everything in writing and make sure details of the meeting are put in your child's file.

How do I keep the line of communication open?

Tip:
Take a Dictaphone to any meeting with the school, so you can record what's being said. Ask first if they don't mind.

The last thing you want is to go to all that time and effort to visit the school and tell them about the bullying, only to feel like they've forgotten about it. To prevent that from happening know when and whom to contact to get an update on what they've done. You also need to know who to speak to so you can tell them whether their measures have stopped the bullying. If they haven't you can ask them to take a different approach.

What do I do in the meantime?

Get your child to keep a bully diary. I can't stress the importance of this. You need well-documented examples of what has been going on.

How do I get the school to do something without becoming a pest?

The most important thing to do is not to let the school off the hook. Keep writing to them, phoning them up and asking for further meetings. Make a nuisance of yourself. Who cares if they have you down as a bit of a pest? Getting the bullying to cease is all that you want. You are not being unreasonable.

What to say

Sometimes schools don't take bullying seriously. What can you do or say to ensure that they do take bullying seriously?

- Don't start by blaming the school and saying 'you should be doing this/you should be doing that'. Coming across as confrontational won't help anyone least alone your child. Schools don't like bullying either.

- Play on the emotional angle. Use descriptive and emotive language to describe the effects of the bullying. Tell the school about the times your child wakes you up screaming. Highlight the alienation your kid feels. An example could be, 'I read my child's diary and she said she felt so alone that she wanted to kill herself.'

- Be polite but assertive making sure the school knows in no uncertain terms that the bullying has to stop. Make it a matter of 'we can do this' and not 'you will do this'. Nobody likes to be dictated to.

The school says...

Schools aren't always as quick to admit their failings as we'd like. Sometimes they trot out the same old excuses. Be prepared for them.

'This school operates a no-blame bullying policy.'

This means that rather than blame the bully the school prefers to try and get them to see the error of their ways using their peers. This no-blame policy might seem weak to some parents, because, let's face it, when your kid is being bullied you have every right to be angry with the bully, but this approach has met with some success.

Ask to see the policy the school has and if you are not satisfied by what it says the school will do, insist that you would prefer it if this situation was handled a different way i.e. the bully was made to realise that their actions won't be tolerated rather than being allowed to come to that conclusion themselves.

'The person you say bullied your child has a good school record and comes from a good family.'

This panders to the myth that most bullies are delinquents. Your reaction could be, 'I'm not saying they're not smart and come from a dysfunctional family, just that they are bullying my child.' Don't get personal: state the facts.

Tip: Empathise with the school. Say, 'I know it must be hard to be responsible for all these children' and, 'I appreciate your time'.

'There is no bullying problem at this school.'

I call this the ostrich manoeuvre, where the school would rather bury its head in the sand than admit that there's a problem. The best thing to do here is not to get into an argument, but to merely state that your child is being bullied and that's a problem to you and should be to the school.

'Your child is oversensitive.'

Usually this plays along the lines of, there's no bullying from what I can see 'just a bit of mucking around' or 'good-natured banter'. You have to be calm at this point even though inside your head you're probably screaming at what's been said. Explain calmly and rationally that you know the difference between the kidding on that goes on between kids and the kind of bullying that reduces your child to tears and makes them have maudlin thoughts.

**Tip:
Remember you can block email addresses and phone numbers if need be.**

In the case of cyberbullying...

Some bullies may not simply be content to target people at school; they may target them at home too. If it's a pupil or pupils at your child's school who are behind the cyberbullying, do tell the school.

There are other things you can do to prevent the bully getting to your child using technology:

- Always approach the website concerned. Contact the moderators and explain what is happening. Ask them what they can do to stop it. They may also be able to delete offensive comments.

- Find out if there is a 'report' button or one for 'abuse'.

- If this fails, block that particular site in your home. If you don't know how, then ask your Internet provider for advice.

- Make copies of offensive comments and emails. Use your screen print function on your computer and print copies for the school. It should be on the top line of your keyboard and say something like 'prt sc' on the key. Then paste to the programme 'Paint' (you'll find it in Programs).

Summing Up

When you send your kids off to school you think they are going into a safe environment where they can learn. Discovering otherwise means that you have to revise that view and do something to get the bullying to stop.

Depending on the school, that can be an easy process or an almighty struggle that will have you in despair. Never fear though, because help is at hand. Schools have policies to deal with bullying and by law they have to implement them.

If they fail in that duty of care to your child there are other things you can do. See chapter 7 to find other avenues you can go down to get the help you need.

Other Help You Can Get

You've told the school about the bullying and they've 'done what they can'. Hopefully the measures they have taken will have worked and your child will be back to their good old selves, but what if the bullying has continued?

Don't despair because the school isn't your only chance of resolving the situation.

Bullying outside school

We've already looked at the fact that schools may refuse to take any responsibility for the bullying your child suffers out of school because legally they are not duty bound to do anything. So what then if the bullying takes place on the school bus or anywhere deemed to be outside school property?

Of course, you should tell the school about the bullying that's happening on the bus, and anywhere else for that matter, although they may not feel compelled to do anything about it. It varies from school to school whether they act. If a school takes bullying seriously they will, at the very least, look into the matter and may even put teachers on bus duty or at the school gates to supervise pupils. If they refuse to do this, point out that the school is meant to look after its pupils because it has a moral responsibility to do so.

Bullying on the school bus

You should approach the bus company and inform them of what's going on. The last thing that any bus company wants is to have the bad publicity of child passengers being injured on one of their buses, especially if they need the schools' contracts as many of them do. They also don't want the driver to have any distractions whilst they are driving in case they crash.

Tip:
You could speak your child's friends and ask them to look out for them on the bus.

What the bus company can do:

- They may insist that teachers ride on the bus if there is bullying on it or they will stop doing the bus run.

- Inform the police and say that they will use CCTV evidence to ensure that kids who misbehave are prosecuted.

- If there is a community police officer they may ask them to come onto the bus to speak to pupils.

- They can even withdraw the bus pass that the bully has if they find out they are harassing people on the bus.

- In severe cases they may opt to stop driving kids from a particular school if the bullying problem is so bad. One bus company I read about did that when pupils tried to shove a boy out the emergency exit of the bus whilst it was still moving.

- If the Local Education Authority (LEA) rather than a public bus service provides the bus, you can complain to them too and ask that your child be seated near to the driver. Be warned, although this may stop bullying on the bus, requesting this may set your child apart from other kids as well as taking them away from their friends. It may be best to find an alternative way to get them to school even if it means driving them there yourself or asking someone you know who does the school run to drive your kids with theirs.

Talking to the bully's parents

In an ideal world it would be a case of knocking on the parents of the child who's been bullying your child's door and telling them what's been going on. They'd be appalled at their child's behaviour and vow to put a stop to it as you sipped tea from their best china whilst seated on their sofa and nibbling on a digestive biscuit.

This is far from an ideal world and you may find that the parents of bullies insist that their little perfect princess or prince 'wouldn't do that' and oh your child must be 'oversensitive' to mistake a 'little leg-pulling' for bullying.

You only have one chance to approach the bully's parents, so try and do it the right way.

There are certain things you have to take into account before you approach them:

- Do you know them well enough to have a friendly chat? What kind of people are they? Are they reasonable? If they have a bad reputation you may be best steering clear.

- Can you trust yourself to control your temper and not be confrontational? If you can't, don't go. Getting into an argument will be of no help to anyone and may make things worse.

- Are you the kind of person who is frank, or are you someone who has difficulty in getting your point across? If you're a bit of an introvert you could end up feeling like you've been run over by a steamroller in any conversation you have with the bully's parents.

- Will you be able to explain calmly and clearly what has been happening without making any judgements? You have to be able to put yourself in the other parents' shoes. If someone came round to your house shouting the odds and accusing your child of picking on other kids, you would go on the defensive too.

- Would it be better if you were to meet the parents in a meeting organised by the school? That way it would be in a controlled environment that you and they would be less likely to find intimidating.

Meet the parents

If you feel that going ahead and speaking to the bully's parents is the best course of action, you have to be careful about how you go about it and what you say:

- Plan exactly what you are going to say. Go there and 'um' and 'ah' and you'll get nowhere. You have to take control of the situation.

- Don't go alone. If both parents are present there's more chance of a successful resolution.

- Don't just barge into their house. If possible contact them first by phone or pop round asking for a suitable time to chat.

- Don't be confrontational. This includes no demanding to see the 'bully'. One of the main reasons that people shouldn't approach bully's parents directly is because too often it ends with the parents at each other's throats and can even lead to violence.

- Empathise with them and the situation they find themselves in. Think of how you would feel if you were told your child was a bully. They may have no indication of what their child has been up to. Don't be surprised if they tell you that their child has suffered from bullying too because often bullied children go on to bully themselves.

- Expect them to go on the defensive. Wouldn't you if someone came over to your house and told you that your child was bullying other children?

- Listen to what they have to say and don't talk over the top of them. The key to a successful resolution is good communication.

- Try and come to some kind of decision about what's going to happen.

- If the talks are fruitless make sure that they know that you will still press ahead with getting the bullying to stop under your own steam.

- Try and keep the lines of communication open. Give them your telephone number and ensure they know they can call you.

- If the situation looks as though it may be set to get violent, leave immediately.

Tip:
Do you have proof that identifies their child as a bully – an email with their address on, a copy of a post on a message board that identifies them?

Find out if any other children are being bullied at the school

- They always say that there's more strength in numbers and they are right. If you find out that other children are being bullied meet with their parents. Together you can demand the school takes action.

- Find out if there is a bullying culture at the school. You could place an ad with a PO box number in your local paper or put an ad in the library. Word of mouth is good too. Make sure that everyone knows that what they tell you will be treated in the strictest of confidence.

Does your school have a PTA or a board of governors?

You feel like you've hit a brick wall with the school, but do you know any of the PTA members/governors? Find out and bring the matter up with them.

Tip:
Go online and look at other bullying websites. Is there anything other parents did to get the bullying to stop?

Go to the Head's boss

I have a friend who goes right to the top to complain about bad service or products she pays for and always with satisfying results.

- In the case of a school failing in its duty to stop your child being bullied you can go over the school's Head and write to the Local Education Authority (LEA).

- You can also contact the education welfare officer there and explain the situation to them asking them to intervene. If you're unhappy with their response, contact the Local Government Ombudsman who can look at the LEA's role in dealing with your complaint. Ask your local council for details.

- Contact the Education Minister at Westminster.

Contact the police

If your child has been assaulted or had anything stolen, it's imperative that you go to the police because whoever is responsible has committed a crime.

- Even if your child has no willing witnesses, the police may still speak to the bully.

- Having police involvement will also help in your case against the bully because they will have a record of being called out that you can use.

- In severe cases you can try and take out an order banning the bully or bullies from coming within close proximity to your child. You will need substantial proof of bullying to convince a judge.

Getting your local councillor/MP involved

Go to your councillor or MP's local surgery. Alternatively you can write to them and request a meeting.

Tip:
Ask other people about the school and their impressions of it.

Write to the Children's Commissioners

Wales were the first to appoint one but there are also individual ones for children in England (there the post is called the Minister for Children), Scotland and Northern Ireland. Contact details are in the help list at the back of this book.

The legal route

This is not to be recommended, as it's very rare that a case succeeds and it's also a very long and drawn out and expensive process that can go on for years. You will also need an abundance of evidence to prove the school was aware of what was going on and failed to act.

Evidence could include a doctor's letter, details of school and police involvement, a report from an educational psychologist on the effects of the bullying, photographs of any injuries they sustained etc.

The first step is to speak to a lawyer who will talk you through what they can and cannot do and the likelihood of a successful lawsuit. If you are on a low income you may get legal aid.

If this all sounds too daunting a prospect, you may find that simply getting a lawyer's letter sent to the school may stir them into taking some action.

Use the media

Tell your story and this may shame the school into doing something. Your best bet is to contact your local newspaper. There should be a telephone number that you can call the news desk on.

Be warned – they will want to send round a photographer and to speak to your child.

Threaten to take your child out of school

This is the last resort. Speak to the school about it. This may spur them into doing more.

If it doesn't, there are two options open to you:

Find another school

- Contact the head teacher of the school that you want your child to go to and see if there are any places available.
- Ask to go in and speak to them directly so that you can explain about the problems you are having at your child's current school.
- Find out what their bullying policy is and how effective it is. If the Head doesn't seem to be that forthcoming then be wary of sending your child to that school. Remember, most schools that deny they have a bullying problem are usually the ones that do have one.

Teach your child at home

Sometimes parents feel that the best thing to do is to teach their kids at home.

Before you commit yourself to home schooling, look at the practicalities. Most importantly do you have the time with your other commitments? Is there a place where your child can work unhindered? How will it impact upon the rest of the household?

For more in-depth advice about homeschooling see the help list at the back of this book.

Tip:
Go down the media route only when all other avenues have failed.

Summing Up

You've been to the school and still the bullying carries on:

- Know that you have other options and so does your child.

- Ensure that your child knows that, because children who are being bullied can slip into a pit of despair when they find that telling you about the bullying hasn't acted like a magic wand and got the bullies to just disappear.

8

Inside the Mind of a Bullied Child

We've looked at stopping the bullying in the previous two chapters, but that isn't all that you can do. There are other ways to help damaged children and we can make a start on that in this chapter.

We first have to fully understand how bullying has affected them, including the thought processes that children go through when they are bullied and what the after effects of the inner turmoil they go through are. Once we fully understand that, we are more capable of empathising with them and helping them to come to terms with what has happened to them so we can undo some of the damage.

The different stages that the bullied child goes through

Bullied children go through a whole raft of emotions and they are mainly negative ones that they can turn inward on themselves. That's why bullying is so psychologically damaging.

The mental process

- Disbelief – They can't believe that this is really happening to them.
- Denial – They feel that it can't be happening to them. That they must be imagining it or being oversensitive.
- Realisation – This is happening.
- Blame – They blame themselves, thinking they must have done something to cause/deserve it or it wouldn't be happening.
- Anger – They become angry with themselves.
- Shame – They feel ashamed that they have 'allowed' this to happen.
- Isolation – They feel marked out as different and alone.
- Terror – Constant fear that it's going to happen again.

The psychological scars

It's no wonder, with the turmoil that bullied children go through often on a daily basis, that the psychological effects of bullying run deep, leaving mental scars. Unlike physical scars these take a long time to heal and sometimes in extreme cases will never fully heal. I can vouch for that.

It wasn't being punched in the stomach that hurt me the most when I became the target of a particularly vicious teenage boy when I was at school, it was having him saunter up to me on the school bus and spitting 'Ugly' in my face in front of everyone. Even today, I am insecure about my looks. That happened over twenty years ago now and I still remember it like it was yesterday. Sometimes, I even think I can still feel the spittle on my face as my tormentor screamed his insult at me.

Tip:
It may help your child to write their feelings down in a notebook that only they have access to. Writing things down helps get the feelings out.

That's one of the main things that parents may not realise about bullying when it's their child on the receiving end. That it's not just a matter of feeling like dog doo when it's happening, but the effects can be long-lasting. Your child may look like they're doing okay, but inside it may be a different story.

Of course I'm an adult now and supposedly older and wiser and maybe I should be able to brush all of the insults and blows I took under the carpet, but somehow I'm not quite there yet. If I feel this bad many years on, just think how bad your child may feel if they are being tormented now.

Why the effects of bullying never end

Being bullied strikes right at the core of who you are. You believe that there is something wrong with you. This has to be because what's happening to you isn't happening to everyone else. You are the one who makes you different, so it must be you.

If you ask most people who have suffered from bullying in their lives they will tell you the same thing, that it's the mental effects of bullying that stay with them. This may be down to the fact that broken bones and cuts heal, but wounds to the mind run deeper and are hidden; no one can see them so they are less easy to deal with.

Why bullying can cause so much psychological harm

Psychologists believe that each individual is a product of their environment and experiences. If you are someone who lives in an environment of fear where you are being made to feel small, that experience starts to mould you, making you do things that you otherwise wouldn't do if you weren't being bullied.

- You may start to walk with your head down and back bent, terrified of making eye contact with anyone because you become convinced that it's you looking at the bully or coming across as cocky that starts it off or that someone will see it as you challenging them and start on you too.

- You may stop answering questions in class because 'swots' or 'teachers' pets' always get bullied.

- You may stop going out with your friends or walking the dog and become reclusive because you are worried that you might bump into your tormentors.

Tip:
It may help your child to write their feelings down in a notebook that only they have access to. Writing things down helps get the feelings out.

- You may become jumpy and paranoid that the bully is going to start on you today, putting you in a constant state of fear and alarm even when nothing is happening.

- You might find yourself being conditioned to behave in a certain way that you feel will lessen your chance of being bullied that day.

The reason this happens and victims of bullying modify their behaviour in reaction to what's happening to them is down to one thing: they blame themselves for the bullying and believe that if they modify their behaviour it will stop. When this doesn't work they turn all of that anger inward.

Again it's their fault that they're being bullied. They should have nipped it in the bud. They should stand up for themselves. Notice, it's all on them and not the bully.

Tip:
You can make sure your child knows bullying is a cowardly thing to do by commenting when it comes up in their favourite TV show or soap.

My experience

Everything that I did when I was being bullied was governed by what was happening. How I walked. How and when I talked – I have a speech impediment which means that I can't pronounce my rs and ls properly, something that I inherited from my mother. This caused a great deal of hilarity amongst my peers, even when many of them couldn't string two words together. I lived in constant fear even when I got a brief respite from the bullying. It would happen at school, on the bus and outside my home. Nowhere was safe and even if it was I didn't feel safe.

Adult bully survivors

To truly understand how bullying can have such long lasting effects the best people to talk to are adult bully survivors. These are people who have been there and know what it's like.

'Many years ago now I was bullied at secondary school and so ashamed that I couldn't tell anyone, not even my parents. It left me wishing that I had never been born. Even now there are days when I think about what happened to me and I still feel the same way.' Simon.

'The bullying I suffered took many forms. It started off as name-calling and being sent to 'Coventry' by the group of girls I used to hang about with who turned against me. Then it escalated to the point where I was being hit with books and people's fists almost every day at school. I used to be a happy child with a lot of spirit, but that was soon knocked out of me. That was thirty years ago and I am now a complete introvert. I have no friends and only my kids and husband keep me going.' Cathy .

'I lost a piece of me when I was repeatedly bullied over two years and I never got it back. My parents got the bullying to stop by taking it up with the school and pestering them, but the effects still remain. People don't realise that once the spirit is taken out of you it's difficult to get it back. I have friends who were bullied who seem to be okay now. I will never be.' Anne.

'What happened to me made me feel so bad that I used to hurt myself in an attempt to get out of going to school. I would shove my hand down my throat and make myself sick, punch myself in the stomach and then complain of tummy ache. Once I even threw myself down the stairs. My parents just thought I was clumsy. They never asked why. I don't have any kind of relationship with them now. I feel that they betrayed me by not cottoning on to what was happening.' Kirsty.

'Bullying at school has led to me becoming so meek that I get bullied at work too. I feel so weak and relive the hell every day in flashbacks. When it happens people look at me like I'm schizophrenic.' Irene.

Tip:
It may help if you can get someone who was bullied to talk to your child about it, making your child feel less alone.

Bullied children's fears

Bullied children fear many things:

- They will always be bullied.

- They'll never make friends again.

- They'll always carry the stigma of being bullied.

- They'll be labelled a grass if they tell about the bullying.

- That the insults the bullies sling at them are true.

- The bullying will never end.

How to get your child to express their feelings

Bottling up feelings is detrimental to anyone. You need your child to open up, something which may not be easy.

- Try some role-playing where you replay incidents of bullying and switch roles. This gets them to express their feelings and helps you to understand how it feels.

- If they can't talk to you, get them an appointment with a school guidance teacher or your family GP and perhaps they will be able to talk to them.

- Ask them to write down things that have happened in a poem, short story or an essay. Even if they don't want to show it to you, putting your thoughts down on paper helps our brains to digest them. For younger children, ask them to draw you a picture.

Tip:
You can help your child with this exercise.

- There are bully charities who have forums especially for kids. Perhaps your child could talk about their feelings on one of them? Children can email ChildLine about anything. The email will go to a trained counsellor. To do this visit www.childline.org.uk. Go to 'Talk' on the links bar at the top and select and scroll down to 'ChildLine email'. Click on 'ChildLine email' and get writing. You will also notice a message board. Like the email function this is for children only and not parents – anything that a child tells ChildLine is in complete confidence. This is vital because the charity also helps children who may be being abused by the very people supposed to take care of them. ChildLine also have online chat for children to use. Users need to register.

Things that helped me... from the mouths of the bullied

I learnt a technique later in life that I wished I'd used when I was being bullied, that you may find useful too:

- I'd write down details of a negative experience that had happened to me as soon as I could get the time to do it so it was fresh in my mind.

- I'd write down how it made me feel.

- Later, I would analyse the situation and say to myself, 'If I told someone about what had happened, how would they interpret it?' or, 'If this happened to someone else and they told me what happened, how would I interpret it?'

- Second time round, I usually found that I'd interpret the incident completely differently and more positively than I did initially.

This method is particularly good for the bullied child because often, when bullying happens, they respond by thinking negatively about themselves rather than the bully.

For example, for a bullied child the incident could be – 'I was picked on today by the bully who punched me. This was my fault because I shouldn't have smiled'.

Looking at the incident later the child may write: 'Everyone has a right to smile if they want. The person who hit me is nothing but a coward and a bully'.

Things that helped me...

- I'd write stories where the bully got their comeuppance or realised their behaviour was a disgrace and begged me to forgive them.

- I'd write witty comebacks to their put-downs.

- I used my brother's punch bag and took my anger out on that.

- I became vegetarian. Believing in something made me feel proud of myself and helped my self-esteem.

- I began going to football matches. When I was watching my team, Dundee United, I forgot all about how miserable the bullying had made me.

Summing Up

By far, the worst effects of bullying are the psychological effects. Helping your child to overcome them is vital to their recovery.

In the next chapter I will suggest ways that you can help your child to improve their shattered self-esteem. This is just as important as getting the bullying to stop.

9

Boosting Your Child's Self-esteem

You can always spot a bullied child. They tend not to make eye contact or smile, and walk around with their shoulders down trying not to attract attention. Their backs are all tense and every movement can seem like it takes great effort. They have cripplingly low self-esteem.

Why self-esteem is important

Good self-esteem is something we all need because if we don't feel good about ourselves then nobody else will. Having good self-esteem makes us believe that we can do things. In a child, that's vital to help them flourish and to grow into the happy, confident adults they are capable of becoming.

A child with good self-esteem will be focused and enjoy life, greeting every day as a new challenge.

A child with poor self-esteem will have little sense of direction and be miserable with every day being seen as something to dread.

Repairing damaged self-esteem

The good news is that it is possible to make your child walk tall again, although it will take time, patience and a whole lot of perseverance, but it will be worth it in the end.

Think of self-esteem as a block of bricks. Bullying takes away some of the bricks at the bottom and they come toppling down. In order to get the self-esteem back you have to start rebuilding that wall and the only way to do that is a brick at a time.

Confidence-building exercises

Try rebuilding your child's shattered self-esteem using a series of confidence-building exercises. The aim of these exercises is to make your child feel good about themselves again.

Please remember, part of having confidence is feeling that you have the right to say no. For that reason your child's participation in these exercises must be voluntary. Make sure that they know you are doing this for their benefit and not for yours.

Exercise one

Help give them a sense of worth – Children who have undergone some kind of psychological trauma such as bullying tend to have a distorted view of themselves and their worth. In this exercise we help them to see themselves as the wonderful human beings they truly are by highlighting their good points.

- Give them a sheet of paper and ask them to do two columns. One with the heading 'personality' and the other with 'appearance'. Note – I know that we should be stressing that it's the inside that counts, but no one wants to think of themselves as ugly and that's how bullied children often think about themselves.

- Now ask them to write down what they like about themselves under both categories. This can be anything from saying they are kind to saying they have nice hair.

What to expect:

- They will probably feel negative about both aspects of themselves.

- If they seem stuck help them out. Say something along the lines of, 'You are always helping your sister with their homework that makes you kind' or, 'Other people would love to have your hair.'

- Think about what they are good at and incorporate those things in the personality column. Are they the one who always waters the plants when you forget? Do they cheer everyone else up when they are feeling down? Do they look after their younger siblings? Anything goes here as long as it makes them think positively about themselves.

Once they've finished:

- Take a look at what they have written (it may be best to do it whilst they are out the room in case they get embarrassed).

- Go through the list and discuss every good point they have written adding in things that you think should be there and giving examples to back it up. This will help them to imprint your positive points in their mind.

- Stress that the good points they have picked up about themselves are also how others see them and that they shouldn't listen to anyone who says otherwise, especially their tormentors.

Exercise two

Encourage social interaction – Bullied kids tend to want to hide themselves away, so encourage them to take up a new hobby that involves as least one other person. This encourages them to socially interact instead of making them awkward as many bullied children are.

This could mean:

- Taking up karate or another martial art. This will have the dual role of making them feel better about defending themselves if the occasion arises and will also help them to make new friends.

- Joining a dance class. And, no this isn't just for girls.

- Taking up a musical instrument. Finding or developing a new talent helps build self-esteem as well as keeping them busy and giving them less chance to think.

- Getting singing lessons. What kid hasn't fantasised about being a pop star? Look in your local paper for singing teachers. They may not be as expensive as you think. Would joining a community choir be a possibility?

- Is there a youth theatre or acting workshops, specifically aimed at kids, near you? Acting is great for helping to bring kids out of themselves and youth theatre/workshops offer the perfect friendly environment.

- If your child is so shy that sending them to a class is out of the question then why not just try inviting one or two of their friends around and getting a movie and snacks in for them? This way they get to have fun in a safe environment and their pals may return the favour and invite them over to theirs.

Tip:
Make sure your child takes part in family decisions like what TV to buy.

Exercise three

Alter what happened to them – After each encounter with a bully, the victim often wishes that they could have handled the situation better. With this exercise they get to do exactly that – in their head or on paper.

Here's how it's done:

- Your child writes down details of an incident that happened. Perhaps the bully let forth with a stream of abuse whilst others looked on and your child's face crumpled. Or maybe the bully tripped them up and they went flying as everyone howled with laughter.

- They write down what they would have liked to have said or done. For the above example it could be that they laughed and said out loud, 'Hey, what's his problem?'. The tripping incident could involve making a quip about 'taking a trip' and flashing a smile. Disarming the bully with humour and making onlookers laugh 'with' you rather than 'at' you is an excellent tool.

Note: The knack of this exercise is to come up with solutions that make them feel better without them turning into a bully themselves, so no physical violence. The whole point of this exercise is to show your child that they can turn the tables on the bully without copying their antisocial behaviour.

Exercise four

Help them to come up with their own happy song – This will be a song that makes them feel happy no matter where they are that they can easily hum in their head for an instant happy feeling. Confide in them what yours is.

Tips for choosing the song:

- It can be a chart-topper that you could pay for them to have downloaded as a ring tone onto their mobile.
- The song may be one that made them happy when they were little perhaps that you used to sing to them.
- The song could be connected to a happy time in their lives, say a family wedding, a birthday party or maybe their favourite film.
- If they can't think of one have a look together. You could do this on the Internet, go into a music store and let them listen to some tunes or talk about their favourite films and theme tunes.

Exercise five

Help them to feel good about themselves. Ask them to make a list of the things they don't like about themselves. Then they have to turn everything they don't like about themselves into something a bit more positive with your help.

For example, if they say that they hate the way they are terrified of going to school every day and they feel like a coward for being scared, you could write in the opposite column that are proud that despite how terrified they are they still went to school, which shows they have guts.

Suggest that they carry this list around with them to look at when they feel down. If they are worried about someone seeing it suggest that they memorise it instead.

They could try using the good things about themselves as positive affirmations to be repeated last thing at night or first thing in the morning. For example, they could look in the mirror whilst brushing their teeth and say 'I have a nice smile.' Saying that will make them smile.

**Tip:
Make sure you mention your child's good points as often as possible.**

Exercise six

Do fun things together. This is what I call the 'Happy Stuff' exercise:

- Draw up a list and get your child to choose one thing every day to do.
- The list could include things like watching an episode of their favourite show, playing a computer game together, having a family karaoke competition, going on a day trip anywhere they want or taking them shopping for something they want.

Exercise seven

Treat your child like an adult whenever you can:

- This could mean getting them involved in the decision-making in the house or in adult-type activities like cooking or gardening.
- Talk to them as if they are another adult not a child and respect their views no matter how much you don't agree with them. This will show that you respect and trust them.
- Always ensure that you make good eye contact and give them your full attention. Think of how you feel when you are talking to someone and they are not listening to you. Your child shouldn't have to feel that way.

**Tip:
They could
have their
happy song
programmed to
wake them up
on their iPod.**

Exercise eight

Teach your child how to walk tall – Good posture makes you look and feel confident.

Try this:

- Get them to stand with their feet together. Now ask them to pull their shoulders back and upwards. Then to pull in their tummy muscles. Hey presto, we have instant confidence.
- Turn it into a fun exercise by pretending to be a catwalk model to illustrate. Play music if it helps.

Other things you can do

- Say something positive every time they make a negative comment about themselves. Be wary that they are not copying your negative language. Negativity is often passed down from parent to child without the parent even realising.

- Stop them from using phrases like 'I can't', 'I'm not good at' and 'I hate myself when'. Make them aware when they are using them. Don't use these phrases when referring to yourself either.

- Be there to listen whenever they want to talk even if it means letting them send you a text message when they're in school and you're at work.

- Do fun things together, not necessarily as parent and child but as friends.

- Always give them something to look forward to.

- Try and provide them with a stress-free home. This will help them to feel that their home is a haven and not somewhere where they have to hide from even more tension.

- Make sure they realise you have confidence in them. This in turn gives them confidence in themselves. Say things like 'thank you', 'please', 'you'd be doing me a big favour if you helped me with the dishes' and 'I'm proud of you'.

- Try not to get angry even when they do something that annoys you. This may trigger bad memories about the bullying. Instead be rational and calm and explain why you are upset. This could be something like, 'I'm upset that your room isn't tidy, because I want you to have a nice room with nice things.'

Tip:
Asking your child their opinion will make them feel valued.

Summing Up

- Your child's confidence has taken one almighty knock, but it is possible to build it back up a step at a time.

- Do it as a team and involve the whole family.

- Just think of self-esteem and confidence as a bridge that has been knocked down. It can, and will, be rebuilt. Believe that and your child will too.

Help List

Although the organisations listed also help and advise parents, there may be occasions where it is the child themselves who can go to them for help. Where this is the case it has been noted.

When children do make contact, anything they say is treated with complete confidentiality by the trained counsellors they may speak or write to. This is important, because without that promise children may not seek help.

Advisory Centre for Education (ACE)

Advisory Centre for Education (ACE), 1c Aberdeen Studios, 22 Highbury Grove,
London N5 2DQ
ACE General Advice: Freephone 0808 800 5793 (Mon–Fri 10am-5pm)
Exclusions Advice: Freephone 0808 800 0327 (Mon–Fri 10am-5pm)
Exclusions Information: 020 7704 9822 for a free exclusions advice pack
(24hr answer phone)
www.ace-ed.org.uk
enquiries@ace-ed.org.uk (note – email advice can only be given to those with a disability that prevents them from using the phone)
An independent advice centre for parents, offering information about state education in England and Wales for 5-16 year olds. They offer free telephone advice.

Beatbullying

Beatbullying, Rochester House, Units 1, 4 & 5, 4 Belvedere Road, London, SE19 2AT
Tel: 0208 771 3377 (main switchboard)
www.beatbullying.org
info@beatbullying.org
You can follow Beatbullying on Twitter @Beatbullying. Beatbullying are also on Facebook and have videos on YouTube. The UK's leading anti-bullying charity, they were given the royal seal of approval when the then soon-to-be royal bride Kate Middleton named them as one of the charities she'd like her wedding guests to donate to.

ChildLine

ChildLine, Freepost NATN1111, London E1 6BR

Tel: 0800 1111 (for children to call)

For parents worried about their child, ChildLine asks them to contact the NSPCC Helpline on 0808 800 5000

www.childline.org.uk

Children's charity, ChildLine offers a free 24-hour helpline for children in distress or danger. Trained volunteer counsellors comfort, advise and protect children and young people who may feel they have nowhere else to turn. They also have information sheets online you can print out as well as a comprehensive list of contact numbers for ChildLine offices throughout the UK.

ChildLine Scotland

In Scotland, the ChildLine service is delivered by Children First for the NSPCC. They have three different offices in Aberdeen, Edinburgh and Glasgow.

They have a special freephone bullying line, which is funded by the Scottish Government and which operates every day of the year, including Christmas – Tel: 0800 44 11 11

www.children1st.org.uk/services/18/childline-in-scotland

Children's Commissioners

Children's Commissioner for England – Maggie Atkinson

The Office of the Children's Commissioner, 33 Greycoat Street, London, SW1P 2QF

Tel: 020 7783 8330

www.childrenscommissioner.gov.uk

info.request@childrenscommissioner.gsi.gov.uk

You can follow Maggie on Twitter @ChildrensComm

Children's Commissioner for Northern Ireland – Patricia Lewsley

NICCY, Millennium House, 17-25 Great Victoria Street, Belfast, BT2 7BN

Telephone (028) 9031 1616

www.niccy.org

info@niccy.org

You can follow Patricia on Twitter @nichildcom

Children's Commissioner for Scotland – Tam Baillie

Commissioner for Children and Young People in Scotland, 85 Holyrood Road, Edinburgh, EH8 8AU

Tel: 0800 019 1179

www.sccyp.org.uk

inbox@sccyp.org.uk

You can follow Tam on Twitter @RightsSCCYP

Children's Commissioner for Wales - Keith Towler

Note, they have two offices – Oystermouth House, Charter Court, Phoenix Way, Llansamlet, Swansea, SA7 9FS

Tel: 01792 765600 Fax: 01792 765601 Fax: 01792 765601

Penrhos Manor, Oak Drive, Colwyn Bay, Conwy, LL29 7YW

Tel: 01492 523333 Fax: 01492 523336

For advice phone: 0808 801 1000 or text free on 80800

www.childcom.org.uk

post@childcomwales.org.uk

You can follow Keith on Twitter @childcomwales, and on Bebo (see site for app)

The Children's Legal Centre

The Children's Legal Centre, Wivenhoe Park, University of Essex,
Colchester, Essex CO4 3SQ

Tel: 01206 877 910

The Children's Legal Centre, 38 Great Portland Street, London, W1W 8QY

Tel: 0207 5801 664

Helpline No: 0808 802 0008 (Mon–Fri 9am–5pm only)

Note: advice given relates to English and Welsh law only.

www.childrenslegalcentre.com

Follow them on Twitter @CLCUK

They offer free legal advice covering all aspects of the law affecting children and young people and free fact sheets. This service is open to children and parents. They have two addresses and although their telephone numbers
are listed, they advise anyone wanting urgent legal advice to call the
helpline number.

The Department of Education

Department for Education, Castle View House, East Lane, Runcorn, Cheshire, WA7 2GJ

Tel: 0370 000 2288

Typetalk:18001 0370 000 2288 (this is a type to voice service for those who unable to use a standard phone)

www.education.gov.uk

The Department for Education is responsible for education and children's services. They have publications on a variety of education-related topics and advice on bullying. Just go to the top left hand corner and put 'bullying' in the search box or homeschooling.

Education Otherwise

Tel: 0845 478 6345

www.education-otherwise.org

A UK-based membership organisation, they provide support and information for parents who homeschool their kids. You must, however, be a member.

Family Lives (England only)

Tel: 0808 800 2222 (the Parentline is free to call)

www.familylives.org.uk

A charity that offers advice to anyone parenting a child. See website for contact details of their 7 different offices. They also offer live chat and textphone support.

The Home Education Advisory Service

Tel: 01707 371854

www.heas.org.uk

A national home education charity, they champion a parent's right to educate their children at home and have a very useful FAQ section. Visit the home page and click on FAQ on the menu down the right hand side.

Home Education

www.home-education.org.uk

The frequently answered questions section is particularly helpful, but applies mainly to England and Wales.

Kidscape

Kidscape, 2 Grosvenor Gardens, London, SW1W 0DH

Phone: 020 7730 3300 Fax: 020 7730 7081

Helpline: 08451 205 204

www.kidscape.org.uk

National charity that's been helping to eradicate bullying and child abuse for twenty years. For advice you must phone up to speak to a trained counsellor.

Local Government Ombudsman
England

The Local Government Ombudsman, PO Box 4771, Coventry CV4 0EH

Tel: 0300 061 0614 8:30 am–5pm Mon–Fri (contact this no to find out how you complain or use the online complaint form by going to the home page and clicking on 'contact us' then selecting the 'complaint form' that's highlighted in blue).

www.lgo.org.uk

advice@lgo.org.uk (for general enquiries only)

Scotland

Scottish Public Services Ombudsman, Freepost EH641, Edinburgh, EH3 0BR
Tel: 0800 377 7330
Fax: 0800 377 7331
www.scottishombudsman.org.uk
You can also visit their offices in person. It's open from 9am – 5pm every weekday except Tuesday when it opens later at 10am.

Wales

Public Services Ombudsman For Wales, 1 Ffordd yr Hen Gae,
Pencoed, CF35 5LJ
Tel: 01656 641 150
Fax: 01656 641 199
www.ombudsman-wales.org
ask@ombudsman-wales.org.uk

Northern Ireland

The Ombudsman, Freepost BEL 1478, Belfast, BT1 6BR
OR this address – The Ombudsman, 33 Wellington Place, Belfast, BT1 6HN
Tel: 0800 34 34 24
www.ni-ombudsman.org.uk
ombudsman@ni-ombudsman.org.uk
If you have a complaint about the education that your child is receiving and your local education authority doesn't deal with it in the manner you think they should, the ombudsman is the person you should contact. All of the websites listed have helpful 'how to complain' sections that explain the process.

Especially for kids

In addition to the websites listed in the help list, there are also websites specifically aimed at children and young people who have been or are being bullied.

Cyberbullying UK

www.cyberbullying.co.uk
This is a great site that offers advice on how to stay safe online in sites such as Facebook, Twitter, YouTube and Bebo amongst others. An essential read for kids and their parents.

National Society for the Protection of Children

www.nspcc.org.uk/homepage2/bullying.htm
The kids' zone has brief down-to-earth advice on bullying.

Net Bullies

www.netbullies.com
This is a site that looks at the issue of Internet bullying in a clear way.

Pacer Centre's Kids Against Bullying

www.pacerkidsagainstbullying.org
Although based in America, the advice offered applies to bullied children everywhere.

Stop Bullying

www.stopbullying.gov
This site run by various government agencies, offers advice for children whether they are being bullied, have seen bullying or have been called a bully.

Note: Please note websites rarely change their addresses, but contact details are subject to change at any time. The inclusion of any organisation in this list is not an endorsement of any kind.

Book List

Creating Kids Who Can
Jean Robb & Hilary Letts, Hodder & Stoughton, 1996, £6.99

Don't Sweat The Small Stuff for Teens
By Richard Carlson, Hodder & Stoughton, 2000, £8.99

How to Talk So Kids Will Learn: At Home and At School
By Adele Faber & Elaine Mazlish, Picadilly Press, 2003, £11.99

Positive Parenting: Raising Children with Self-Esteem
By Elizabeth Hartley-Brewer, Cedar Books,1994, £10.99

Smart Thinking: Confidence & Success Sorted
Frank McGinty, Piccadilly Press, 2001, £5.99

Lightning Source UK Ltd.
Milton Keynes UK
UKHW050646281018

331342UK00003B/75/P